Ecology
and Conservation

M. J. Reiss and J. L. Chapman

Series editor
Fred Webber

CAMBRIDGE
UNIVERSITY PRESS

PUBLISHED BY THE PRESS SYNDICATE OF THE UNIVERSITY OF CAMBRIDGE

The Pitt Building, Trumpington Street, Cambridge CB2 1RP, United Kingdom

CAMBRIDGE UNIVERSITY PRESS

The Edinburgh Building, Cambridge CB2 2RU, United Kingdom

40 West 20th Street, New York, NY 10011-4211, USA

10 Stamford Road, Oakleigh, Melbourne 3166, Australia

First published 1994

Third printing 1998

Printed in the United Kingdom at the University Press, Cambridge

A catalogue record for this book is available from the British Library

ISBN 0 521 42158 6 paperback

Designed and produced by Gecko Ltd, Bicester, Oxon

This book is one of a series produced to support individual modules within the Cambridge Modular Sciences scheme. Teachers should note that written examinations will be set on the content of each module as defined in the syllabus. This book is the authors' interpretation of the module.

Cover photo: Kenya Wildlife Service annual Ivory burn, Nairobi National Park (Hadley/Greenpeace Communications)

Acknowledgements

Illustrations and data

Table 1.2 from Whittaker, R.H. (1975) *Communities and Ecosystems*, 2nd edn, Collier Macmillan, London; table 1.3 from Krebs, C.J. (1978) *Ecology: The Experimental Analysis of Distribution and Abundance*, 2nd edn, Reprinted by permission of HarperCollins College Publishers, fig. 1.4 from Schmidt-Nielsen, K. (1983) *Animal Physiology: Adaptation and Environment*, 3rd edn, CUP; fig. 1.7 from Whittaker et al (1973) 'Niche, habitat and ecotope', *American Naturalist* 107, 321–38, University of Chicago Press; fig. 2.4 from Dempster J.P. (1975) *Animal Population Ecology*, Academic Press, London; fig. 2.5a and b and fig. 2.6 from Gause G.F. (1934) *The Struggle for Existence*, Williams and Wilkins, Baltimore, USA; figs 2.9 and 4.7 from Roberts M.B.V., Reiss M.J. and Monger G. (1993) *Biology: Principles and Processes*, Thomas Nelson & Sons Ltd; table 3.1 from Lange, M. and Hora, F.B. *Collins Guide to Mushrooms and Toadstools* (2nd edn), Collins 1965 imprint of HarperCollins Publishers Ltd; fig 3.1 from Jones-Walters L.M. (1989) *Keys to the Families of British Spiders*, *Field Studies* 9, 365–443, Field Studies Council; fig. 3.3 from Williams G. (1987) *Techniques and Fieldwork in Ecology*, Bell & Hyman imprint of HarperCollins Publishers Ltd; fig. 3.4 from Moss, B. *Ecology of Fresh Waters: Man and Medium* (2nd edn), Blackwell Science Ltd, 1988; fig. 3.5 from Chalmers N. and Parker P. (1989) *The OU Project Guide: Fieldwork and Statistics for Ecological Projects*, Field Studies Council; fig. 3.9 from Hawksworth, O.L. and Rose F. (1976) *Lichens as Pollution Monitors*, Reproduced by permission of Edward Arnold (Publishers) Ltd, London; fig. 4.3 reproduced by permission of the University of Cambridge Local Examinations Syndicate; fig. 4.4 from Professor C.D. Keeling, Scripp's Institution of Oceanography, USA; fig. 4.5 from Gribbin J (1988) 'The greenhouse effect', *New Scientist, Inside Science* 22 October, 1–4; fig. 4.6 from J.C. Farman, British Antarctic Survey; fig. 5.4 from the Royal Society for the Protection of Birds; fig. 5.7 from Rowland, M. (1992) *Biology*, Thomas Nelson & Sons Ltd; table 6.1 from Southwood T.R.E. (1961) 'The number of species of insect associated with various trees', *Journal of Animal Ecology*, 30, 1–8 Blackwell Science Ltd; table 6.2 from Dowdeswell W.H. (1987) *Hedgerows and Verges*, Allen & Unwin imprint of HarperCollins Publishers Limited; fig. 6.3 from Moore, N.W. (1983) 'Ecological effects of pesticides', in Warren A. and Goldsmith F.B. (eds), *Conservation in Perspective*, 159–75, Reprinted by permission of John Wiley & Sons Ltd; fig. 6.5 from Cole, L. (1983) 'Urban nature conservation', in Warren A. and Goldsmith F.B. (eds), *Conservation in Perspective*, 267–85, Reprinted by permission of John Wiley & Sons Ltd.

Photographs

1, 20*t*, Biofotos; 3 Silvestris/Frank Lane Picture Agency; 4 Paul Sterry/Nature Photographers; 5 Alfredo Rock/Planet Earth Pictures; 10, 33 Chilworth Meda Associates; 11 Stephen Dalton/Natural History Photographic Agency; 12 Alan Williams/Natural History Photographic Agency; 16 Andrew Syred/Microscopix; 17 Dr J.P. Dempster; 20*b* Martin W. Grosnick/Ardea London; 24 Jeremy Burgess/Science Photo Library; 29 Graham Burns/ Environmental Picture Library; 31 Brinsley Burbidge/ Nature Photographers; 35, 38 John Walmsley Photo Library; 40 Heather Angel/Biofotos; 42 Pilly Cowell/ Environmental Picture Library; 48 Geoscience Features; 50 Bob Gibbons/Ardea London; 55 Joe Blossom/Wildfowl and Wetlands Trust; 57 Pete Addis/Environmental Picture Library; 60 Gardiner/Greenpeace Communications; 63 Guy van Raaij/Environmental Picture Library; 64 John Hammond; 67 Jupiter Urban Wildlife Centre.

Every effort has been made to reach copyright holders; the publishers would like to hear from anyone whose rights they have unwittingly infringed.

Contents

Introduction

This book covers the subjects of ecology and conservation. **Ecology** is the study of organisms in their natural surroundings. The surroundings of an organism are known as its **environment**. Environments consist of many components including both *physical* features, such as climate and soil type, and *biological* features, such as predators and prey.

Conservation refers to the attempts by humans to preserve organisms and environments that are at risk as a result of human activity. But successful conservation requires a knowledge of ecology. That is why this book starts by examining the central concepts of ecology before going on to the issue of conservation.

Ecology comes from two Greek words – *oikos* meaning home and *logos* meaning understanding. So ecology is all about understanding the homes of animals, plants and other organisms. Understanding the ecology of an area is a bit like trying to put together a gigantic multi-dimensional jigsaw. Some of the pieces are the individual species in the area, for example earthworms, bluebells, oak trees, marbled white butterflies, wood ants and wood warblers. Others are the important aspects of the physical environment, for example the pH of the rainwater, the total amount that falls in a year, how it is distributed throughout the seasons, and significant information about the temperature, sunlight and soil type. These various jigsaw pieces interlock with one another in numerous, subtle ways.

Ecologists spend their time trying to take such jigsaws apart and examine them carefully to see how the pieces fit together. If all goes well an ecologist may be able to *predict* what will happen if some of the bits of the jigsaw are removed or damaged, such as if a species becomes extinct or if the rainfall pattern changes.

Having said that, ecology is in many ways the most complicated of all the biological sciences. Ecologists have to know something about the structure, physiology and behaviour of organisms before they can begin to understand how such organisms interact with one another and with the physical environment. For these reasons, ecology is above all an *experimental* science. Ecologists need constantly to test their predictions either in natural environments out in the field, or in artificial, simplified laboratory experiments.

This is why chapter 3 (which sits between chapters on the principles of ecology and chapters on the principles and practice of conservation) looks at *practical* ecology. Theories can be of great value in ecology, but they must always be tested against reality, and this is where practical ecology is so important.

In many ways ecology is a relatively new science. Indeed, the word was only coined by the German biologist Ernst Haeckel in 1869, fully ten years after Charles Darwin published his theory of natural selection. Yet in little over a century it has grown to become one of the most important disciplines within biology. We hope that this short book will serve as a clear introduction to the subject at Advanced Level, and encourage you to study it further.

This book is dedicated

to Stephen Tomkins and John Birks

Chapter one

Biomes, communities and succession

By the end of this chapter you should be able to:

1 explain the meanings of the terms biome, habitat, microhabitat and ecological niche;

2 outline the classification of world vegetation types into biomes;

3 describe the main environmental factors which lead to biomes differing from one another;

4 list the key physical and biological features of the following biomes: tropical rainforest, desert and coral reef;

5 distinguish between an ecosystem and a community;

6 describe the succession from fresh water or bare rock to woodland;

7 explain what are meant by climax community and deflected succession (plagioclimax);

8 make and record observations to investigate succession.

Biomes, habitats and microhabitats

We all use terms such as 'desert', 'tropical rain-forest', 'swamp' and 'coral reef' to classify the biological diversity we see in the world around us *(figure 1.1)*. Terms such as these describe **biomes**. A biome is a natural grouping of organisms occurring over a large area. Other examples of biomes are temperate woodland, tundra, lakes and deep ocean benthos. The last refers to the marine organisms that live on the ocean floor (the benthos).

Within each biome there are many habitats. A **habitat** is the place where an organism lives – the word is a Latin one and literally means 'it dwells'. Organisms of the same species can live in a number of habitats. For example, the common rat (*Rattus norvegicus*) is typically found associated with farms, refuse tips, sewers and warehouses.

However, it also occurs in hedgerows close to cereal crops or sugar beet and in salt marshes. On islands (e.g. the Isle of Man, Rhum and Lundy) it also occupies grassland and the coastline.

With small organisms, especially if they live in a very restricted area such as a particular region of the soil or on a single plant or animal, it is worth being more precise about exactly where they live. The term **microhabitat** – 'a small habitat' – is used to describe this. Just as a single biome has many habitats within it, a single habitat may have many microhabitats.

To illustrate the importance of microhabitats, consider an oak tree. If you are an insect, life is very different depending on whether you live on the upper surface of the leaves, the lower surface of the leaves or inside them. It is even more different if you live under the bark, next to the roots or inside an acorn. Each of these different places is a microhabitat.

● *Figure 1.1* Mangrove swamp, an example of a biome. Notice the aerial roots. These have pores on them that allow oxygen to diffuse in from the atmosphere.

The diversity of biomes

Ecologists recognise some 35 to 40 different biomes, the exact number depending on the classification system used. Terrestrial biomes are generally classified according to the structure of their vegetation (e.g. whether it is forest, scrub or grassland, evergreen or deciduous) and climate (e.g. tropical, temperate, arctic or alpine). A list of those aspects of the physical environment which determine the structure and geographical distribution of terrestrial biomes is given in *table 1.1*.

The vegetation in an area grows to the maximum amount allowed by the environmental conditions. Thus, if rainfall is very low, only a few specialised plants are able to survive and the biome will be desert. The higher the annual rainfall the more lush and taller the vegetation is and the more species there will be in the biome. Sometimes many factors operate together. For example, increased altitude is associated with a shorter growing season, greater variation in temperature, increased ultraviolet radiation and decreased partial pressures of carbon dioxide and other gases – all of which make life more difficult.

Aquatic biomes can be classified according to the nature of their water. Is it fresh, salty or brackish (as in an estuary)? Is the environment stable (as in deep ocean where it is pitch dark and 4 °C) or variable (as in a seasonal mountain stream or tidal shore)? Are there abundant nutrients (as in a coral reef or salt marsh) or very few (as generally in deep ocean)? How much light is there? (Little light penetrates below 30 m in coastal waters and 150 m in open ocean waters.)

We shall now look at three different biomes in more detail. It should be remembered that we are describing *natural* biomes. However, each of these biomes suffers from pollution, habitat destruction and other aspects of human influence, as we shall discuss in later chapters.

Tropical rainforest

Tropical rainforests require a hot climate and abundant rainfall throughout the year. They are found near the equator in South and Central America, West and Equatorial Africa, South-east Asia, Indonesia and North-east Australia. The combination of year-round warmth and moisture allows continuous plant growth to occur. The result is that **plant productivity** is extremely high *(table 1.2)* and the plants tend to be evergreen (they retain leaves throughout the year). High plant productivity and a relatively constant climate result in a tremendous diversity of life. Tropical rainforests have the greatest diversity of life of any of the world's biomes. Most of the species they contain have not even been named, let alone studied.

At ground level some tropical rainforests can be surprisingly easy to walk through. This is because little light reaches the forest floor. Most of it is trapped by the **canopy**, some 30–50 m up, and it is here that the bulk of the photosynthesis occurs.

Many trees in the canopy bear **epiphytes** (plants that grow on other, larger plants) and **lianas** (climbing plants which use the trees to support their growth into the canopy). **Nutrient cycling** within the canopy is important, and many plants possess aerial roots. These absorb water and nutrients, just

Physical features	Examples
climate and weather	temperature (average values, daily range and seasonality) rainfall (total each year, seasonality and pH) light (degree of seasonality)
geology and soil	underlying rock type (e.g. limestone, sandstone, granite) composition of soil (e.g. pH, soil organisms, nutrient content, % clay, silt, sand, humus, water and air)
topography	height and shape of the land distance from sea

● **Table 1.1** Aspects of the physical environment which determine the structure and geographical distribution of terrestrial biomes

Biome	Net primary productivity/ dry g m^{-2} yr^{-1}	
	Mean	Range
tropical forest	2000	1000–3500
swamp and marsh	2000	800–3500
algal beds, coral reefs and estuaries	1800	500–4000
temperate forest	1250	600–2500
tropical grassland	900	200–2000
cultivated land	650	100–3500
temperate grassland	600	200–1500
continental shelf	360	200–1000
lake and stream	250	100–1500
tundra and alpine	140	10–400
open ocean	125	2–400
semi-desert and desert	40	0–250

● **Table 1.2** Net primary productivity (measured as the mass of dry organic matter accumulated per m² per year) in some of the world's major biomes

as soil roots do, and some are even photosynthetic. The nutrients come from plant exudates and from the decomposition of dead animals and their faeces. Many animals spend their entire lives in the canopy. Flowers and fruits are found throughout the year and provide nourishment for countless insects, birds and mammals.

Other animals are specialist leaf eaters (*figure 1.2*). Sloths, for example, have large multi-compartmented stomachs which hold cellulose-digesting bacteria. These enable the sloths to break down tough leaves. Even so, food may spend a month in the stomach before passing into the intestines for absorption. Living on such an

indigestible diet has many consequences for a sloth's ecology. Sloths are, of course, notoriously slow. Their body temperature is low for a mammal, about 30–34 °C, and variable, falling each night, during wet weather and when the animal is even less active than usual. These strategies all help conserve energy. Their slow life-style means they cannot run away from predators or fire. Camouflage is therefore important as an anti-predator device and is provided by two species of cyanobacteria (blue-green bacteria) which live in their fur and turn it green. There are a lot of leaves in a rainforest and the sloth life-style has been very successful – sloths are the most abundant large mammals in tropical South American forests.

Although tropical rainforests are very productive, almost all the nutrients are tied up in the organisms themselves. Decomposition is so rapid that the soils contain little in the way of organic matter or minerals. As a consequence, removal of the vegetation, whether by logging or burning, rarely leads to successful agriculture. Within a few years crops fail and the farmer is forced to clear another patch of land.

Desert

Deserts are dry. Usually they receive less than 50 mm of rain a year. As a result soils are thin or absent (*figure 1.3*). Not

● **Figure 1.2** Three-toed sloth carrying young and eating a thick leaf.

3

● *Figure 1.3* Deserts receive little rain and have little or no soil. Desert plants show various adaptations which allow them to survive for long periods without water. Cacti are visible in this Mexican desert.

only is water scarce in a desert, it is unpredictable. The key to survival is making the fullest use of the rain when it does come. Some plants are **ephemerals**, meaning 'short-lasting'. These plants can complete their entire life cycles within a few weeks. A sudden fall of rain is rapidly followed by germination, growth, flowering and seeding. As a consequence, the fragile soil may be carpeted overnight with flowers to the horizon. As Thomas Gray put it: 'Full many a flower is born to blush unseen, and waste its sweetness on the desert air'.

Other desert plants are **perennials** which survive the long periods between rains as adults rather than seeds. **Geophytes** (literally 'ground plants') survive as underground bulbs or corms, producing their above-ground parts after heavy rain. **Succulents**, such as cacti and *Euphorbia,* have many anatomical, biochemical and physiological adaptations which allow them to persist above ground between rains by minimising transpiration. They owe their name to the fact that they store water in large parenchyma cells, making the plants *succulent*.

Typically succulents have thick cuticles, a very low surface area to volume ratio and sunken stomata. In most cacti the leaves are reduced to defensive spines and photosynthesis is carried out instead by the green stems. In some succulents the stomata only open at night, when water loss is minimised. Carbon dioxide diffuses in and is fixed into malic acid. At daybreak, the stomata close, the malic acid is broken down and the carbon dioxide released within the plant. This carbon dioxide is then joined onto RuBP (ribulose bisphosphate) by the enzyme RuBP carboxylase as in the usual light-independent stage of photosynthesis. Such plants show **crassulacean acid metabolism** and are known as CAM plants. The net result is that these plants grow more slowly, but lose less water, than other plants.

Desert animals too face a number of challenges. Both water and food are in short supply. Daily variations in temperature may be extreme with searingly hot temperatures during the day that plunge at night. There may be blinding sandstorms, and even when there is no wind loose sand can make locomotion difficult.

Animals cope with these difficulties in a wide variety of ways. That archetypal desert animal, the camel (*Camelus dromedarius*), has evolved a number of appropriate adaptations. For a start, camels can survive even if they lose up to 30% of their ideal water content, twice the figure typical of most mammals. When a camel does become short of water, its body temperature fluctuates by up to 7°C (*figure 1.4*). This enables the camel to save water which would otherwise have to evaporate to keep it cool. Contrary to what you might suppose, a camel's fur also helps to reduce water loss. A sheared camel loses up to 50% more water than an unsheared camel. Further adaptations to life in the desert are splayed hooves which make it easier to walk on shifting sand, and a hump which stores fat. Not only is this fat a food store, it also releases water when it is broken down and used as a fuel in respiration.

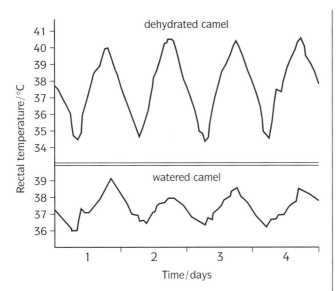

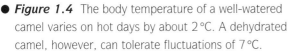

● *Figure 1.4* The body temperature of a well-watered camel varies on hot days by about 2 °C. A dehydrated camel, however, can tolerate fluctuations of 7 °C.

There are not only hot deserts, but also cold ones. The south polar desert valleys in the mountains of Antarctica are barren, dry, snowless places with no visible life, although some fungi and algae live *within* the rocks just under the surface.

Coral reef

Coral reefs are the tropical rainforests of the oceans. They have a wealth of life and a complexity that ecologists are only beginning to unravel. Most people find them stunningly beautiful too. Many species of corals are known, but all are cnidarians

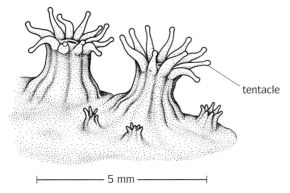

● *Figure 1.5* Corals are composed of individual polyps embedded in a limestone skeleton. Most corals are colonial with polyps averaging 1–3 mm in diameter. This diagram shows part of a coral with two fully grown and three juvenile polyps visible. Each polyp is surrounded by a ring of tentacles.

and related to sea anemones. Reef-building corals are found only in clear seas within 50 m of the surface and where the temperature of the water remains above 20 °C throughout the year.

Most corals are colonial and secrete a protective limestone (calcium carbonate) skeleton into which they can retract when danger threatens. They are both **autotrophic** and **heterotrophic**. Their heterotrophic nature is the more obvious of the two as the individual polyps of which a coral is made have tiny tentacles with which food is caught *(figure 1.5)*. However, the polyps also contain symbiotic, unicellular dinoflagellates. These are autotrophic protoctists which fix carbon dioxide in photosynthesis and are responsible for the high productivity of coral reefs *(table 1.2)*.

A single reef contains an abundance of different species of coral. In turn, these corals support a tremendous variety of other life. The reef provides both a source of food for a large number of creatures and also a home. Some of the fish, such as parrot fish, have powerful jaws. These enable the fish to bite off chunks of coral in order to eat the polyps inside. Polyps are also eaten by a number of invertebrates. Perhaps the best known of these is the crown-of-thorns starfish (*Acanthaster planci*). These are sometimes found in plague proportions, causing devastation to a reef *(figure 1.6)*. It is still unclear whether these occasional population explosions of *Acanthaster* are natural or the result of human disturbance.

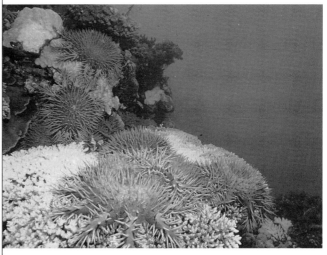

● *Figure 1.6* A group of crown-of-thorns starfish attacking a coral reef in the Red Sea.

Coral reefs cannot survive in muddy water as the corals become clogged with sediment. If rivers carry heavy loads of silt out to sea (because of soil erosion inland) reefs cannot form opposite the river mouths.

Niches

In our descriptions of tropical rainforests, deserts and coral reefs, we have begun to outline some of the ways in which organisms interact with each other and with their physical environment. We have already seen that a habitat is that part of the environment occupied by an organism. A **niche** is a complete description of *how* the organism relates to its physical and biological environment. Just as in a jigsaw puzzle where each piece has its own unique shape and pattern and only fits in one place, so each species has a unique niche – the way it fits into its environment.

Consider a particular species, say the grey heron (*Ardea cinerea*). Its habitats are water meadows, rivers, lakes and the sea shore. A complete account of its niche would include a description both of its physical environment (such as the type of water it needs, the temperature range in which it can survive and reproduce) and of its biological environment (such as the prey it eats, its competitors and the vegetation it needs for its nest).

It is difficult to provide a quantitative description of an organism's niche. *Figure 1.7* shows the feeding niche of the blue-grey gnatcatcher, *Polioptila caerulea*, a North American bird. This is an **insectivore** and the horizontal axis shows the length of the insects on which it feeds. The vertical axis shows the height above ground at which it forages. The contour lines with numbers show the frequency with which the birds feed at a particular height and on a particular length of prey. You can see that the birds concentrate on prey 4 mm in length which they catch about 3–5 m off the ground.

However, there are many other aspects to an organism's niche in addition to its feeding niche. In theory other axes could be added at right-angles to those in *figure 1.7*. Temperature could be shown on a third axis, risk of predation at different times

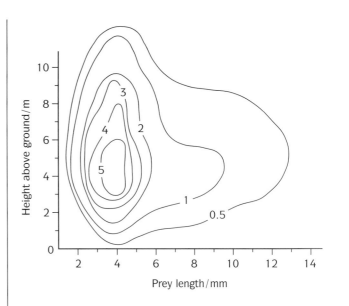

● **Figure 1.7** An attempt to show the feeding niche of the blue-grey gnatcatcher (*Polioptila caerulea*) in two dimensions. The curved contours show the feeding frequencies for adult gnatcatchers during the incubation period in July and August in oak woodlands in California. 95% of the diet is taken within the contour marked 5, 96% within the contour marked 4, 97% within the contour marked 3, and so on.

of the year on a fourth, height above ground of the bird's nest on a fifth, and so on. In practice, no more than two or three axes can be shown on a graph, but computers can nowadays store and compute data for many more.

Each species has its own unique niche

The ecological principle that no two species can coexist if they occupy the same niche is known as **Gause's competitive exclusion principle**. The biologist G. F. Gause gets the credit even though earlier workers had expressed essentially the same idea and even though he never summed up his conclusions as precisely as the competitive exclusion principle now states. What he did do, though, was to carry out in the early 1930s a long series of very carefully planned and recorded laboratory experiments on two closely related species of unicellular ciliates, *Paramecium caudatum* and *P. aurelia*. (These species are protoctists with cilia on their surface.)

Gause found that no matter how often he tried, he couldn't get the two species to coexist in a culture. Gause kept the ciliates in small 5 cm³ culture bottles, in which they fed off bacteria. Kept on their own, each species happily existed for years, reproducing and perpetuating itself. However, when kept together, *P. caudatum* always became extinct within a few weeks. This was not because it was eaten by the other species (*P. aurelia*); it was simply that it reproduced less quickly than *P. aurelia* and eventually died out. *P. caudatum* had been outcompeted by *P. aurelia*, which is why Gause's findings are now known as the competitive exclusion principle.

Gause's work on niches was extended by T. Park in the 1950s. Park worked with two species of flour beetle, *Tribolium confusum* and *T. castaneum*. Again, both types of beetle could be kept apparently indefinitely when reared with others of their own species. Again, when put together, only one species survived. However, Park found that by varying the physical environment in which the beetles were kept, he could determine which species survived and which became extinct. For example, at a temperature of 24 °C and a relative humidity of 30%, *T. confusum* always outcompeted *T. castaneum*. However, at a temperature of 34 °C and a relative humidity of 70%, the reverse was the case. Interestingly, under certain conditions, sometimes one species survived, sometimes the other (*table 1.3*). However, as with Gause's *Paramecium*, only *one* species survived.

The notion that each species has its own niche has been one of the most important principles in ecology. In recent years, however, it has been called into question. For example, consider plants. Most plants need much the same things from their environment: water, carbon dioxide, light, space and nutrients. A British woodland, meadow or grassland contains dozens of different species of plants. Is it really the case that each has its own unique niche?

One possibility is that the answer to this question is 'yes'. After all, even closely related plants have subtle differences in their root

Temperature/°C	Relative humidity/%	% of times T. confusum wins	% of times T. castaneum wins
24	30	100	0
24	70	71	29
29	30	87	13
29	70	14	86
34	30	90	10
34	70	0	100

● **Table 1.3** The result of competition between two species of flour beetle, *Tribolium confusum* and *T. castaneum*, averaged over many replicates in a variety of laboratory environments

systems and the arrangement of their leaves, allowing them to 'specialise', as it were, on different sources of water, nutrients and light. Furthermore, it should be remembered that the competitive exclusion principle refers to the *whole* of an organism's niche. It might be that two closely related species of grass, for example, overlap greatly in the demands they make on the physical environment, yet have seeds that germinate in different circumstances, or are susceptible to different herbivores.

The other possibility is that it is *not* always the case that coexisting species occupy distinct niches. It might be that, in nature, interspecific competition is less important than in Gause's and Park's laboratory experiments. It has been calculated that in some circumstances, the length of time taken for one species to drive another to extinction by interspecific competition is, on average, longer than the typical length of time between speciation events. That is to say, by the time one species has become extinct as a result of the competitive exclusion principle, another one or two species may have evolved to replace it!

Communities and ecosystems

A **community** is an association of species which live together in some common environment or habitat. Most communities are composed of a mixture of prokaryotes, protoctists, fungi, plants and animals. The organisms in a community interact with one another in all sorts of ways. For a start, there will be feeding relationships. In most communities, **autotrophs** (also known as **producers** and comprising green plants, photosynthetic algae, photosynthetic bacteria and chemosynthetic bacteria) provide food for **herbivores** (also known as **primary consumers**). In turn, herbivores are eaten by **first-level carnivores** (also known as **secondary consumers**), and these may be eaten by **second-level carnivores** (or **tertiary consumers**). Eventually organisms die and their remains are broken down by **decomposers**. These feeding relationships can be represented by **food chains** or by **food webs** which show the interrelationships between the various food chains in a community.

The species in a community also interact with one another in other ways. They may rely on one another for reproduction, as is the case in the pollination of insect-pollinated plants. Or one species may act as a home for another – as a humpback whale carries barnacles. Or the interaction may be more subtle – all the species in a woodland, for example, rely on the activities of the various soil organisms which recycle nutrients.

The term 'community' is a valuable one in ecology. However, in 1935 Sir Arthur Tansley invented the term **ecosystem** because he realised that the organisms that make up a community cannot realistically be considered independently of their physical environment. The term ecosystem applies to a community of organisms *and* its associated physical environment.

Consider the rock pool community shown in *figure 1.8*. Any biologist can immediately deduce certain features of the physical environment, for example that the water is salty, just by noticing which species are present. A description of the rock pool ecosystem would include not only a list of those organisms likely to be found there, but also the significant features of the physical environment. In the case of a rock pool this would include knowing how salty the water is, whether the rock pool ever dries out, how often it is diluted by rainwater or covered by the sea, how much the temperature varies each day, and so on.

There is one other feature of ecosystems and their associated communities worth stressing: ecosystems are, to a large extent, self-contained. Indeed, to call a rock pool an ecosystem is to

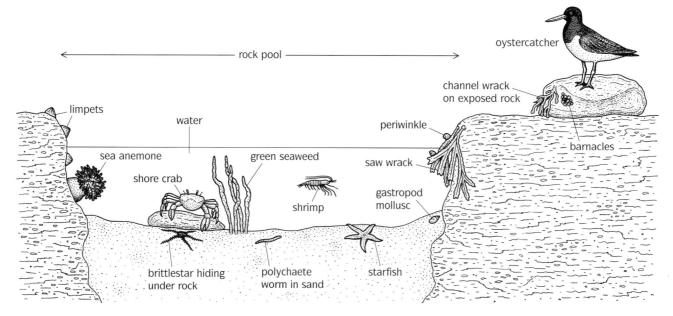

● **Figure 1.8** A cross-section through a typical rock pool in Britain. A variety of species are shown that belong to the rock pool community, together with some organisms outside the rock pool, such as the oystercatcher and polychaete worm, that inhabit other parts of the rocky or sandy shore.

stretch the term somewhat, simply because the small size of a rock pool and its tidal exposure by the sea means that it isn't really that self-contained. Most ecosystems are more self-contained than a rock pool. Even a very small wood can be home to a large number of species, the members of which will typically spend their entire lives in that wood. Nutrient cycling will take place largely within the confines of the wood, and most organisms will show adaptations to the woodland habitat which would make them unsuitable for life in a neighbouring grassland or lake.

SAQ 1.1

Arrange the following terms in a hierarchy of **descending size** and **complexity**: community, ecosystem, biome, habitat, microhabitat.

SAQ 1.2

Suggest **ten** features of the physical environment in a lake which are of significance to the organisms living there.

Succession

Many communities change over time. A natural change in the structure and species composition of a community over time is called a **succession**. This definition excludes changes that are the immediate, direct result of human activity. For instance, changes due to ploughing, tree felling and the planting of crops would all be excluded.

It is often convenient to focus on changes in the vegetation when investigating or describing succession. However, it is important to remember that changes in the animals (not to mention the fungi, protoctists and prokaryotes) will accompany such botanical developments. Changes in the vegetation are often responsible for changes in the other species in a community, so that it makes sense to focus on the plants.

At its most clear-cut, succession starts on bare, uncolonised ground or in newly formed lakes, both of which lack soil or vegetation. The changes that result are known as **primary succession.** Examples of primary succession today can be found in the arrival

and establishment of organisms in such habitats as sand dunes, volcanic lava flows, landslides and the land and lakes left by retreating glaciers.

More often, though, succession on bare ground takes place after vegetation has been destroyed by fire or covered with volcanic ash or flood silt. Under these conditions, there are generally the remnants of soil, even if it is covered by barren, inorganic matter. Frequently too there are buried seeds and sometimes underground animals which can lift buried soil to the surface. Such factors accelerate the pace of succession and may affect its course. Succession in an area that has previously been vegetated is known as **secondary succession**.

Why does succession occur?

Imagine a shallow soil that gradually, over many years, becomes deeper and alters its composition. These changes will be the result of the weathering of the parent rock and of the accumulation of organic matter and nutrients from decaying organisms. Such changes in the soil may mean that the vegetation alters. For instance, a deeper soil may be able to support trees which shade out earlier vegetation, while a soil whose pH has dropped because of acidic leaf litter will support only those species tolerant of acidic conditions. This sort of change in the vegetation – the result of effects caused by the plants themselves – is known as **autogenic succession** ('autogenic' literally meaning 'giving rise to itself').

Alternatively, changes in a community over the passage of time may simply result from some external influence. For example, a lake may silt up with muddy streamwater, or a rise in sea level may flood an area. The ensuing change in the vegetation and other organisms is known as **allogenic succession** ('allogenic' literally meaning 'others give rise to it').

We shall concentrate on autogenic changes, partly because of their intrinsic interest and partly because they often occur more rapidly than allogenic changes. However, over the Earth's history, allogenic changes have been of great importance, as they will no doubt continue to be, even if they often operate over a time span of thousands of years or longer.

Succession from bare ground to woodland

The first organisms on newly exposed bare rocky areas are animals such as spiders which can hide in the cracks between boulders or stones. These animals are carnivores (catching live prey such as insects) or scavengers (feeding off dead organisms). They rely on food being blown in, or on small animals flying in by mistake. As yet there are no plants.

Succession really gets going once autotrophs begin to live in the habitat. Such autotrophs form the base of food chains and the food web, providing food for herbivores. On bare rocky ground the first colonisers are usually lichens and mosses, as these organisms can cling directly to the rock surface *(figure 1.9)*.

With the passage of time, the presence of lichens and mosses helps soil to build up. Such soil is largely the result of the gradual weathering of the parent rock, a process accelerated by the action of lichen rootlets and moss rhizoids on the rocks themselves. Soil formation is also helped by the accumulation of wind-blown particles, trapped by the lichens and mosses. Eventually sufficient soil exists to support the presence of vascular plants, such as ferns and flowering plants.

When the bare ground contains small particles such as silt or clay, colonisation is faster and the lichen and moss stage may be omitted altogether. The presence of the silt or clay allows vascular

● *Figure 1.9* Lichens and mosses – often the first colonisers of exposed rock.

plants to root. From the very first, there will be nutrients available for root uptake, and the young 'soil' will have some water-holding properties but may lack the crumb structure of a mature soil.

Plants with nitrogen-fixing bacteria in root nodules are often among the first plants to colonise an area once soil has begun to build up. Examples of such plants are certain horsetails in the genus *Equisetum*, and the legumes *Trifolium* (clover) and *Lupinus* (lupin). These plants come with a built-in advantage, for their nitrogen-fixing bacteria enable the plants to grow in soils with very low nitrate levels. Plants that lack nitrogen-fixing bacteria, for example grasses, tend to arrive later in the succession.

Eventually in the succession the soil is deep enough to support bushes and trees. The first bush and tree species that establish are likely to have wind-dispersed seeds. A common northern European example is birch (*Betula* spp.). Birch is a pioneer tree and its seedlings require high light levels to establish.

Once a few bushes or trees are established, they form an ideal site for roosting birds. This speeds up the rate at which new woody plants arrive as many such species have seeds that are dispersed by birds. In northern Europe examples of mid-successional bushes and trees that produce fruits or seeds which are eaten (and so dispersed) by birds include hawthorn (*Crataegus monogyna*), black-thorn (*Prunus spinosa*), privet (*Ligustrum vulgare*) and oaks (*Quercus* spp.).

Once woodland is established it may be colonised by more shade-tolerant trees, such as limes (*Tilia* spp.), ash (*Fraxinus excelsior*) and hornbeam (*Carpinus betulus*). By now, we have come a long way from the bare ground with which we started. Over much of England and parts of Wales, western Ireland and southern Scotland, the natural vegetation is mixed deciduous oak woodland containing oaks and other tree species such as ash or birch *(figure 1.10)*. Because this is the typical endpoint of the succession, oak woodland is said to be the **climax community**. In terrestrial biomes different climax communities result from differences in climate and geology.

● *Figure 1.10* A typical mixed deciduous oak woodland showing a wealth of plant life.

Actually, the notion of a 'climax community' can be exaggerated. For example, for reasons which are still not fully understood, oak fails to replace itself in mature oak woodland. For this reason, a shifting mosaic is found in which oak regeneration relies on gaps in the woodland vegetation. Such gaps may result from gales, fires or other natural disasters. It is not therefore the case that a climax community occurs in any one place century after century without change.

A mature deciduous woodland is home to many plants in addition to tall trees. A number of woody plants fail to reach the canopy but exist in a **shrub layer**. These plants include hazel (*Corylus avellana*), roses (*Rosa* spp.) and a different species of hawthorn (*Crataegus laevigata*) from that found earlier in the succession. Then there are the plants found in the ground layer. These may include wood anemone (*Anemone nemorosa*), bluebell (*Hyacinthoides non-scripta*), bracken (*Pteridium aquilinum*) and other ferns, mosses and liverworts.

Accompanying the changes in vegetation as a mature woodland develops are changes in the other organisms. Food webs gradually increase in complexity, and a mature oak woodland supports thousands of different species. Amongst the most obvious are the birds. Some of these birds are herbivores (e.g. finches), others are insectivores, feeding either on aerial insects (e.g. warblers) or on insects and other invertebrates found under bark (e.g. woodpeckers). Then there are the various mammals, ranging in size from shrews, woodmice and voles, through dormice and squirrels to the badger and roe deer.

It is impossible in a book of this length even to begin to describe the variety of invertebrate life found in a mature woodland. The soil alone contains hundreds of different species – including springtails, mites and nematode worms – and then there are all the insects, spiders and other creatures (from tiny thrips to large butterflies) that live above ground. Finally, there are the fungi, whose presence is revealed by their autumn fruiting bodies, and the many protoctists and bacteria. All this abundance of life is the result of autogenic succession on bare ground

Succession from fresh water to woodland

Nothing could be more different than bare rock and open water. Yet over most of Britain the typical endpoint of primary succession on both is the same – mixed, deciduous oak woodland. This is a tribute to the tremendous power of autogenic succession.

The open water of lakes may be colonised by **free-floating aquatic plants**. These float on the surface, for example duckweeds (*Lemna* spp.), or beneath it, for example algae such as *Chara*. At the edges of the lake it will be shallow enough for sufficient light to penetrate to allow **rooted submerged aquatics** such as pondweeds (*Potamogeton* spp.) to grow. The establishment of such plants leads to an increase in the organic matter and nutrients on the bottom of the lake. A shallow mud develops. In time, a small or shallow lake gradually fills in as the remains of dead plants accumulate, their decomposition arrested by the anaerobic conditions of the waterlogged environment.

It is therefore the fate of all but the very deepest lakes gradually to decrease in area and eventually to disappear. Parts of the lake may be shallow enough to allow plants to grow that are rooted in the mud, but have leaves that float. Water lilies (e.g. *Nymphaea* and *Nuphar*) are familiar examples. As the lake becomes shallower, plants such as *Phragmites* (common reed) and *Typha* spp. (reedmaces) invade from the edges of the lake (*figure 1.11*). These plants have creeping rhizomes which trap mud and produce large quantities of **leaf litter** as they die back each winter.

Eventually a layer of dead, incompletely decayed organic matter, known as **peat,** builds up. Once this peat becomes raised above the water surface at dry times of the year the community changes further. The vegetation becomes dominated by sedges (*Carex* spp.). Animals, such as water boatmen, fish and newts, that rely on free standing water throughout the year, disappear. Soon trees such as willows (*Salix* spp.) and alder (*Alnus glutinosa*) invade. If the area dries out further the succession may continue towards the eventual establishment of mixed, deciduous oak woodland.

Deflected succession

Succession does not always proceed right through to the establishment of a climax community. Much grassland, for example, is maintained as such by human activities like burning, mowing or controlled grazing (e.g. by sheep). In the absence of these factors, grassland is usually colonised by scrub and develops into woodland. For this reason, grassland is said to be the result of **deflected succession** and is described as a **plagioclimax.**

Another example of a deflected succession leading to a plagioclimax is a hedge. Hedges are maintained by regular cutting back. A hedge that is left for more than a few years develops into a line of trees. This may have consequences for the smaller plants and other organisms found there as a line of trees provides a different set of habitats from a hedge.

Investigating succession

There are three main ways in which succession can be studied. The most direct is to record the organisms and the physical environment in one location over a period of time, and see how they change. A lawn that is left unmown, for example, might be studied over a period of ten years. By the end of this period, the grass will have changed its species composition considerably. Bushes will probably have invaded with associated changes in the animals present.

The only problem with this approach is that it takes rather a long time. A second approach is to find an example where a number of different stages in the succession are present at any one time close to one another. For example, you might look at the organisms and physical environment on a beach, starting with open sand, continuing through sand dunes and ending up with scattered woodland behind the dunes.

The main problem with this approach is that you cannot be certain that the differences between the various habitats (in this case open beach, sand dunes and scattered woodland) are the result of natural succession. There might be some other explanation.

● *Figure 1.11* A pond in Sussex gradually becoming smaller as a result of succession.

A third approach to the study of succession attempts to get over this problem. It consists of looking at historical records. Old photographs and manuscripts may be valuable, but most important is information left by the organisms themselves. For example, suppose you are studying a woodland at the side of a lake. You suspect that the woodland is the result of succession from open water. By taking soil samples at various depths it may be possible to collect and identify the **pollen** produced by plants. Should you find a regular sequence in the pollen, with woodland plants at the top, reeds and bulrushes further down, and finally no pollen at all still further down, your hypothesis will have received support. Should the soil change from a typical woodland soil at the surface to peat further down to muds still further down, you can be even more confident that succession has occurred from open water to woodland.

SAQ 1.3

Outline an approach you could take to investigate **succession** on cow pats.

Questions

1 Describe the essential features of a tropical rainforest and suggest why this biome is so species-rich.

2 Discuss the problems faced by organisms living in deserts or rock pools.

3 Distinguish between the terms **habitat** and **niche**. How might you investigate the niche of a particular species of garden slug?

4 Explain what is meant by a **deflected succession** and discuss the relevance of this concept to farmers.

SUMMARY

- Biomes are natural groupings of organisms occurring over large areas. Examples include tropical rainforest, desert and coral reef.

- A habitat is the place where an organism lives.

- A niche is a complete description of how an organism relates to its physical and biological environment.

- Gause's competitive exclusion principle states that no two species can coexist if they occupy the same niche.

- A community is an association of species which live together in a common environment or habitat.

- An ecosystem is a community of organisms together with its associated physical environment. Ecosystems are relatively self-contained.

- A natural change in the structure and species composition of a community over time is called a succession.

- Primary succession starts with bare ground or open water, whereas succession in an area that has previously been vegetated is known as secondary succession.

- The endpoint of a succession is known as the climax community. Over much of Britain the climax community is mixed, deciduous oak woodland.

- A community that is prevented by the actions of humans from proceeding to the climax community is said to be the result of deflected succession. It is called a plagioclimax.

Interactions between organisms

1 explain what is meant by a population;

2 describe and explain the features of sigmoid population growth;

3 discuss and give examples of the significance of limiting factors in determining the final size of a population;

4 explain the meaning of the term 'carrying capacity';

5 describe and give examples of intra- and interspecific competition and explain their effects on population size and distribution;

6 discuss the predator–prey relationship of lynx and snowshoe hares;

7 distinguish between symbiosis, mutualism and parasitism;

8 outline the life cycle of the liver fluke as an example of a parasite and with reference to control measures;

9 describe the association between *Rhizobium* and leguminous plants as an example of mutualism.

Populations

A **population** is a group of individuals within a species that have the opportunity to breed with one another because they live in the same area. It follows from this definition that individuals from two different species cannot belong to the same population. This is because, with occasional rare exceptions, species are **reproductively isolated** from one another. Tawny owls do not breed with short-eared owls, for example.

Any one species is divided into many populations which are geographically separated. Bluebells in one wood, for example, will belong to a different population from the bluebells in another wood several kilometres away. Indeed, in a large wood there could be several populations of bluebells, though the boundaries between populations may be somewhat arbitrary.

Population growth

Imagine a newly formed volcanic island, and suppose that succession has reached the point where there are several plant species with large numbers of herbivorous insects feeding off them. As yet, though, there are no birds. Now suppose that a few individuals of an insectivorous bird species arrive. They may die out, but alternatively they may succeed in breeding. At first a graph of population size against time drawn for this bird species will show a **lag phase**. During this time the birds are adjusting to their new environment prior to reproducing.

With the passage of time, the number of individuals increases rapidly. The population is said to show **exponential growth**. During this time it grows **geometrically**. This means that the time taken for the population to double in size is constant. Suppose, for example, that each year the population increases by a factor of four, meaning that the doubling time is six months. If the exponential phase starts with a total of 10 birds, there will be 40 birds after one year, 160 after two, 640 after three, 2560 after four and slightly over 10 000 after five.

Clearly this cannot go on for ever. For a start, the amount of food and nesting space on the island will not be infinite. This means that there will be **competition** for resources that are in limited supply. This competition is **intraspecific** because it occurs between individuals belonging to the same species. The result of this increasing competition is that the population growth slows down. Eventually the population reaches the maximum size that the environment can sustain, a figure known as the environment's **carrying capacity**.

These stages in the growth of a population apply to most species of organisms. The stages are shown in *figure 2.1*. Of course, this graph is idealised. In reality there are fluctuations about this smooth curve. The curve shown in *figure 2.1* is known as the **sigmoid growth curve** because it is 's'-shaped (*sigma* is the Greek equivalent of s).

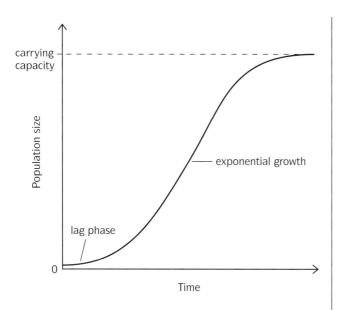

● **Figure 2.1** A generalised graph showing population size as a function of time. Much the same shape is seen whether population size is plotted linearly on the vertical axis, or logarithmically. One advantage of plotting the vertical axis on a logarithmic scale is that the exponential phase falls on a straight line between the lag phase and the point at which population growth starts to slow down.

Measuring population growth

The simplest way to quantify population growth is to count all the individuals in a population as the population increases in size. This method is only really possible when the organisms are easily seen and not too numerous, and when the generation time is not too long. For example, it is feasible to count the number of *Lemna* (duckweed) individuals on the surface of an aquarium or small garden pond during the course of a few months in the summer. However, with smaller organisms, such as bacteria or yeast, some sort of sampling method is needed.

When studying such populations, samples need to be taken at regular intervals. For bacteria the easiest approach is to use **serial dilution**. In this technique, each sample, once taken, is diluted 10 times, 100 times, 1000 times, 10 000 times and so on. Each of these progressively more dilute samples is then plated out, using standard micro-biological techniques, onto a petri dish containing nutrient agar. The petri dishes are then incubated,

usually at 30 °C, for a few days and the number of bacterial colonies counted. It is assumed that each colony has developed from a single bacterial cell. What one finds is that at some dilutions there are simply too many colonies for their number to be counted accurately. At the other extreme, there are dilutions at which no bacterial colonies are found. However, at one of the intermediate concentrations somewhere between 3 and 30 colonies will be found, a number that can be counted precisely. The dilution and volume used for this sample are known, so the bacterial population size in the original colony can be calculated.

To give an example, suppose you want to count the number of bacteria in 500 cm³ of milk (just under a pint) whilst going stale *(figure 2.2)*. At each sampling date, take just 0.1 cm³ from the milk bottle and mix it thoroughly with 9.9 cm³ of sterile distilled water. Label this mixture '×5000' (because 0.1 cm³ is one-fivethousandth of 500 cm³). Then take 0.1 cm³ of this mixture and spread it out onto a petri dish labelled '×500 000'. This is because if you multiply the number of bacterial colonies observed after a few days by 500 000 (i.e. half a million) you will get an estimate of the number of bacteria in the original 500 cm³.

What often happens is that there are still too many bacteria in the ×500 000 sample. As a result, the colonies merge into one another and cannot be counted. For this reason, the best thing to do once you have prepared the petri dish labelled '×500 000' is to take a further 0.1 cm³ of the mixture labelled '×5000' and mix it thoroughly with 9.9 cm³ of sterile distilled water. Label this new mixture '×500 000' (why?). Then take 0.1 cm³ of this mixture and spread it out onto a petri dish labelled '×50 000 000' (why?). Then take a further 0.1 cm³ of the mixture labelled '×500 000' and mix it thoroughly with 9.9 cm³ of sterile distilled water. Finally, label this new mixture '×50 000 000' and take 0.1 cm³ of it and spread it out onto a petri dish labelled '×5 000 000 000'.

The chances are that, once they have been incubated for a few days, you will be able to determine the number of bacterial colonies on one of these three petri dishes. By taking new samples from

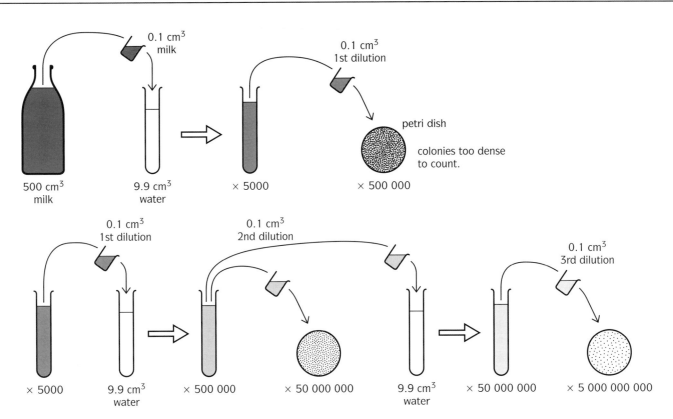

● *Figure 2.2* An example of serial dilution in practice. This procedure can be used to determine the population size of very small organisms such as bacteria or yeasts.

the original milk bottle every 12 or 24 hours you will be able to find out how the bacterial population changes with time. As the numbers of bacteria increase you may find that you need to dilute your sample still further, producing a fourth petri dish at each sampling time labelled '×500 000 000 000'.

Yeast cells are larger than bacteria, so they can be counted directly under a microscope using a **haemocytometer**. This is a special slide with a large number of squares ruled onto it *(figure 2.3)*. The smallest of these squares are a twentieth of a millimetre on each side. This means that their surface area is $0.05\,mm \times 0.05\,mm = 0.0025\,mm^2$. When the coverslip of the haemocytometer is in place, the distance between its lower surface and the ruled surface of the haemocytometer is a tenth of a millimetre. This means that the volume of fluid above one of the smallest squares is $0.0025\,mm^2 \times 0.1\,mm = 0.000\,25\,mm^3$. As a result, counting the number of yeast cells seen above one of these squares and multiplying by 4000 (1 divided by 0.000 25) gives you the number of yeast cells in the population per cubic millimetre.

SAQ 2.1

Suppose that a pair of brown rats is introduced to an island, and that each year over a period of ten years the population size is measured to be 2, 8, 55, 330, 2000, 7500, 9000, 8000, 9500, 8500. Determine the **doubling time** during the period of exponential growth and the **carrying capacity**.

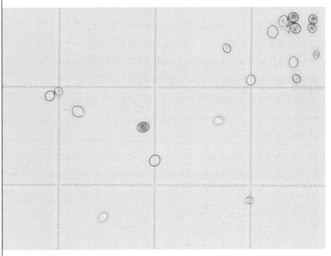

● *Figure 2.3* A haemocytometer with yeast cells as seen under the light microscope. Each of the complete squares visible is $0.05\,mm \times 0.05\,mm$.

Competition in a plant bug and its prey

Anthocoris sarothamni is a small predatory plant bug, related to the bed bug. Its habitat is a plant called broom (*Sarothamnus scoparius*), and the adult bugs are about 4–5 mm in length. *Anthocoris* individuals are carnivorous and obtain most of their nutrients and energy from two species of a smaller bug, *Arytaina* (*A. spartii* and *A. genistae*). In years where there are large numbers of *Arytaina*, the reproductive success of *Anthocoris* females is high – they lay more eggs. It seems that there is **intraspecific competition** among *Anthocoris* individuals for food.

Broom plants vary greatly in the number of *Arytaina spartii* individuals found on them. Research by J. P. Dempster has shown that the greater the number of adult females, the fewer the number of eggs they each lay (*figure 2.4*). *Arytaina* females lay their eggs in the stems of the new growth of the host plant (broom). What seems to happen is that the more *Arytaina* females there are, the greater the competition among them for suitable **oviposition sites** – places where the females can lay their eggs.

The data in *figure 2.4* provide strong evidence that intraspecific competition is taking place between *Arytaina spartii* individuals for oviposition sites. Of course, there might be another explanation. Just because there is a negative correlation between the number of *A. spartii* females and their reproductive success does not *prove* that intraspecific competition is involved. Some ecologists have argued that the only way to prove that intraspecific competition is responsible is to alter the number of individuals in a population and see the consequences.

SAQ 2.2

If intraspecific competition is responsible for the relationship seen in *figure 2.4*, what effect would removing half the adult females prior to oviposition have on the average number of eggs laid by **each** of the remaining females?

SAQ 2.3

How would you expect the **total** number of eggs laid by the females to change?

Limiting factors

Something that prevents a population from increasing in size is called a **limiting factor**. We have just seen that a limiting factor for *Arytaina spartii* is the number of oviposition sites available for the females, while a limiting factor for *Anthocoris sarothamni* is food. At any one point in time, there is usually just one limiting factor for a population. However, different limiting factors can operate at different times. The most important limiting factor is often food, but water, space, specific nutrients and nesting sites can also be limiting factors for animals. For plants, the main limiting factors are light, water, carbon dioxide, temperature, space and the right conditions for germination.

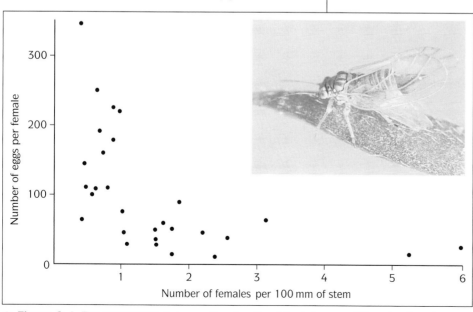

● *Figure 2.4* The relationship between the density of *Arytaina spartii* females (one is shown in the inset) and the number of eggs each lays.

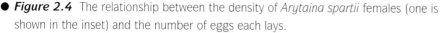

17

Competition in *Paramecium*

Interspecific competition, that is, competition *between* species, is difficult to demonstrate in nature and ecologists vary in the importance they think it has. Some ecologists believe it plays almost no role in the functioning of communities. Most, however, believe it is sometimes important, though probably less so than intraspecific competition.

We have already referred to a classic demonstration of interspecific competition in a laboratory environment (see pages 6–7) when we looked at Gause's discovery that two species cannot coexist indefinitely in the same niche. It is worth examining Gause's data again.

Gause worked with two unicellular organisms belonging to the genus *Paramecium*. When grown on their own, both *P. caudatum* and *P. aurelia* showed typical sigmoid growth curves (*figures 2.5a and 2.5b*). When grown together, however, although the two species could coexist for a while (*figure 2.6*), *P. caudatum* always eventually became extinct.

An objection that can be raised against Gause's work is that it was carried out in the laboratory. His data show that, under laboratory conditions, interspecific competition is indeed extremely important; so important, in fact, that the presence of *P. aurelia* always drove *P. caudatum* to extinction. But we are left with the question: how important is interspecific competition in nature? We shall now look at the evidence for interspecific competition between red and grey squirrels.

Competition between red and grey squirrels

The red squirrel (*Sciurus vulgaris*) is native to Britain. The larger grey squirrel (*S. carolinensis*) was introduced to Britain in the last century from North America. Over the last 150 years the grey squirrel has spread throughout much of Britain. At the same time, the red squirrel has greatly reduced in range and numbers.

The question is whether red squirrels have suffered at the hands of grey squirrels as a result of interspecific competition. The answer certainly seems to be 'yes'. Grey squirrels don't attack reds, but they are twice as heavy and always win in competition for scarce, valuable food sources. The red squirrel also seems to have been unlucky, in that its numbers were probably considerably reduced last century as a result of disease. This allowed the grey squirrel to get a toe-hold into the red squirrel's niche.

However, all is not lost for the red squirrel in Britain. Although much of the country now lacks red squirrels and is dominated by greys, red squirrels are found in places such as the Isle of Wight, where the grey squirrel has never reached, and in conifer woods. Indeed, red squirrels outcompete grey squirrels in woods provided that at least 75% of the trees are conifers (such as pine) rather than hardwoods (such as oak or beech). In other words, Britain is probably big enough for red and grey squirrels to coexist indefinitely. The single niche originally occupied solely by the red squirrel seems to have been subdivided into two niches. In one of these the grey squirrel is the more successful; in the other the red squirrel emerges victorious.

Population cycles in lynx and snowshoe hares

The story of the red and grey squirrel shows how the numbers of one species can affect the numbers of another as a result of interspecific competition. A much more direct way in which the numbers of one species can affect the numbers of another is seen when one species is a predator and the other is its prey.

The Canadian lynx (*figure 2.7a*) and the snowshoe hare (*figure 2.7b*) provide an example of a **predator–prey relationship**. Annual records of the numbers of lynx and snowshoe hares trapped in northern Canada have been kept since the 1820s by the Hudson's Bay Company – a company that trapped animals for their fur. What the trappers found was that the numbers of lynx went through a ten-year cycle. At the peak of the cycle thousands of lynx would be caught in a season. Five years later, at the trough of the cycle, despite all their

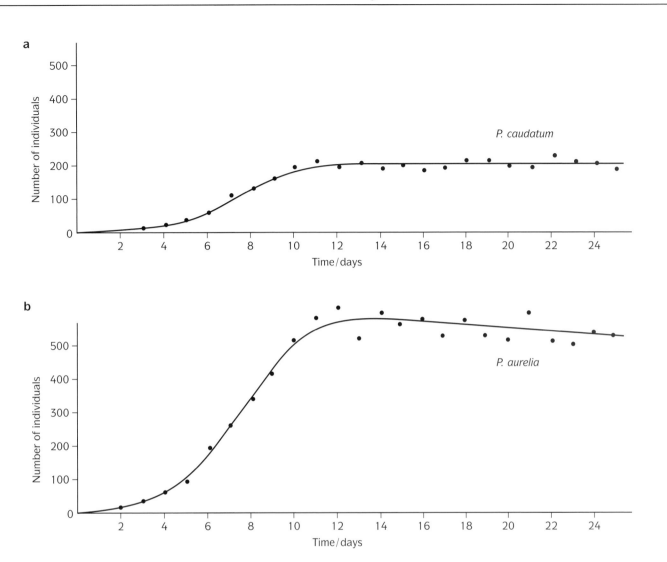

● **Figure 2.5** **a** The population growth curve of *Paramecium caudatum* maintained on its own in a laboratory culture by Gause. **b** The population growth curve of *P. aurelia* maintained on its own in a laboratory culture by Gause.

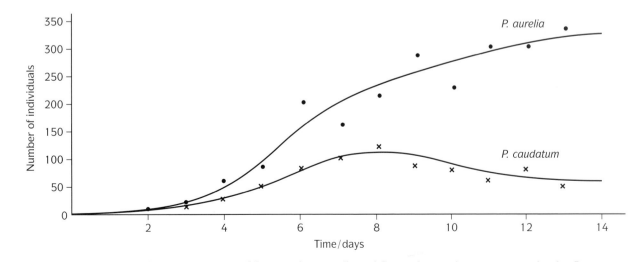

● **Figure 2.6** The population growth curves of *Paramecium aurelia* and *P. caudatum* when grown together by Gause. Eventually *P. caudatum* always became extinct.

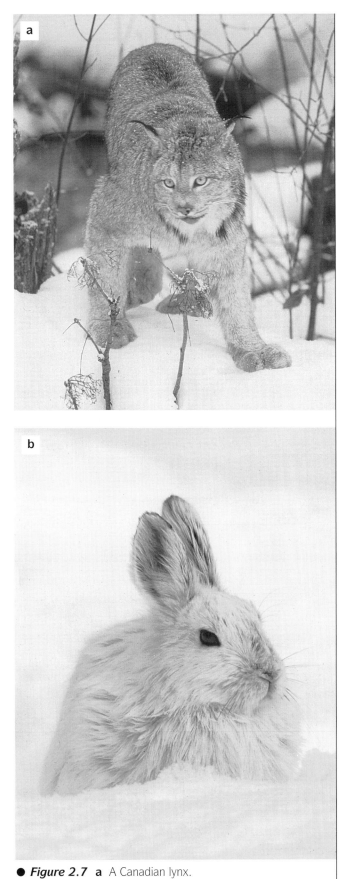

● **Figure 2.7** **a** A Canadian lynx.
b A snowshoe hare in its winter coat.

efforts the trappers could manage at most only a couple of hundred lynx.

Why do lynx numbers fluctuate so greatly, and so regularly? When it was realised that their main prey, the snowshoe hare, also goes through the same ten-year cycle *(figure 2.8)*, biologists thought that the two cycles might be linked. The following chain of events could explain the fluctuations.

- Low lynx numbers mean that few hares are caught by the lynx. As a result, the hare population increases greatly.
- The large population of hares allows lots of lynx to survive and reproduce. As a result, the lynx population increases greatly.
- The population explosion of lynx means that they eat so many hares that the hare population crashes.
- The shortage of hares leads to starvation amongst the lynx. As a result, the lynx population crashes.
- The low lynx numbers mean that few hares are caught. As a result, the hare population begins to build up and the cycle starts again.

There is only one thing wrong with this explanation for the cycles of lynx and hare numbers. Some islands off the east coast of Canada have hares, but no lynx. On these islands, the hares go through exactly the same ten-year cycles as the hares on the mainland! In other words, it doesn't look as though the lynx are causing the population cycles of the hares, but the hare population cycle may still be causing the changes in lynx numbers.

Exactly what is going on is still uncertain. Many small herbivores, not only snowshoe hares, cycle in numbers. Examples include lemmings and, in Britain, short-tailed field voles. It may be that changes in plant abundance and quality cause fluctuations in the populations of the herbivores, such as snowshoe hares, that depend on them. Or it may be that at high densities herbivores become stressed and so breed less well. In any event, it does seem to be the case that cycles in the numbers of herbivores cause fluctuations in the numbers of their predators. In northern Canada lynx cannot easily switch to another food source as there are

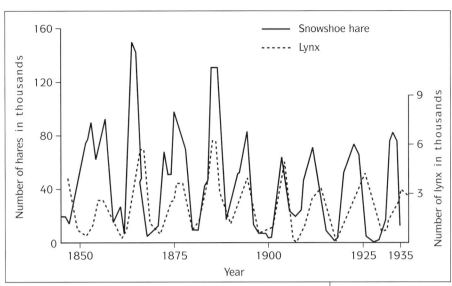

● **Figure 2.8** The relationship between the numbers of lynx (predator) and snowshoe hare (prey) between 1845 and 1935 as shown by the number of animals trapped by the Hudson's Bay Company.

few species of herbivore in the harsh environment. This is why their numbers are so dependent on the numbers of snowshoe hare.

Human population size

So far in this chapter we have looked at the consequences of competition and predation for population biology. Yet the title of this chapter is 'Interactions between organisms' and organisms interact in all sorts of ways other than competition and predation. However, before going on to look at some of the other ways in which organisms interact with one another, it is worth looking briefly at the growth of the human population.

In 1994 there were some 5.5 billion people alive in the world. That's five and a half thousand million of us. Every day the number increases by about 250 000. In other words, each day a quarter of a million more people are born than die. We in the West are used to thinking that this is a problem of developing countries. It is true that most industrialised countries, such as the UK, the USA and France, have population growth rates that are low compared to those in other countries. Bangladesh's population, for example, is growing 12 times faster

than that of the UK. Yet the average person in the UK contributes 40 times as much carbon dioxide to the atmosphere, and hence to global warming, than the average person in Bangladesh. So the present level of population growth in the UK can be argued to be more harmful to the Earth's ecology than the far higher level of population growth in Bangladesh.

Recently the population biologist David Richardson has tried to calculate the carrying capacity of the UK for people. The current population of the UK is 57 million, but to feed this population we have to import a large proportion of our food. Under intensive cultivation, agricultural self-sufficiency could support around 41 million people. In other words, given a population of 41 million we should be able to provide all our nutritional needs, provided we carried on farming intensively using fertilisers and pesticides. A less intensive use of our land, which might prevent the net loss of soil through soil erosion, would probably mean a population of at most 35 million.

So the carrying capacity of the UK from the point of view of our food may be somewhere between 35 and 41 million people. However, for us to be able to rely on renewable energy sources (wind, solar, tidal, wave and geothermal) rather than on fossil fuels (coal, gas, oil, peat) or nuclear power would probably require us to reduce our population to some 15 to 20 million.

Such a reduction may seem far-fetched, though it is interesting to note that only immigration is preventing the populations of many industrialised countries (such as Germany and Italy) from falling. It has been argued that the quality of life would be much better in the UK if there were only half or a third the number of people there are today. Imagine if this were the case. There would be less pollution, more room for wildlife, and no more traffic congestion.

Symbiosis, mutualism and parasitism

The general term given to a close relationship between individuals from two species is **symbiosis** (literally 'living together'). At one extreme, symbiotic relationships can be ones in which both species benefit. Such relationships are said to be **mutualistic**. At the other extreme are relationships where one species lives at the expense of the other. **Predation** occurs when the species that benefits (the **predator**) is bigger than the other (the **prey**). A predator kills many prey during the course of its life. **Parasitism** occurs when the species that benefits (the **parasite**) is much smaller than the other (the **host**). A parasite generally lives on or in only a few host individuals during its life, and often does not kill them.

We shall look first at the liver fluke as an example of a **parasite**, and then at the association between the bacterium *Rhizobium* and leguminous plants as an example of **mutualism**.

The liver fluke

The liver fluke *Fasciola hepatica* is a flatworm in the phylum Platyhelminthes. Its life cycle is shown in *figure 2.9*. The adult fluke lives in the bile passages of sheep. Here it reproduces sexually, producing enormous numbers of offspring, an adaptation seen in many parasites. The parasite needs to produce so many offspring because the chance of any one of them developing to sexual maturity is extremely small.

The fertilised eggs are deposited in fields in the sheep's faeces and a small larva emerges from each egg. This larva, known as a **miracidium** (plural **miracidia**) larva, moves by means of cilia. These enable it to swim through thin films of water. If the miracidium larva is lucky, it chances upon an amphibious snail and penetrates its fleshy foot. In Britain the most significant snail in the liver fluke life cycle is called *Limnaea truncatula*. The snail is said to be the fluke's **secondary host**, its **primary host** being the sheep (or occasionally cattle). The snail can also be considered as a **vector** that carries the flukes from one sheep to another.

Once inside the snail the liver fluke goes through a complicated series of changes before attacking the snail's liver. Eventually a large number of **cercaria** (plural **cercariae**) larvae are produced by asexual reproduction. These usually move towards the mantle cavity of the snail – its gaseous exchange surface. From here the cercariae leave the snail via its pulmonary aperture.

Having left the snail, the cercariae swim towards blades of grass. Here they form **cysts** and go into a **dormant stage**. As a cyst the liver fluke can survive for up to a year. Eventually, if it is fortunate (and a sheep less so) the cyst is ingested by a grazing sheep. The cyst successfully resists the host's digestive enzymes and opens to release a small, sexually immature fluke. This moves from the sheep's gut to its liver. Once in the liver, the fluke gorges itself and grows to sexual maturity, so completing the life cycle.

Controlling liver flukes

Liver flukes can have a serious effect on the health and productivity of sheep, even killing them. As with most parasites, there are several ways to control liver flukes. The key is to prevent successive generations of the parasite from completing their life cycle. In the case of the liver fluke, the following approaches can be taken.

- Treat infected sheep with chemicals, a practice known as **chemotherapy**. A number of different chemicals are used, many retailing under commercial rather than scientific names.
- Move sheep around from one pasture to another, a practice known as **pasture rotation**. The principle behind this is that the cysts from the cercaria larvae are either not ingested before they die of old age or are ingested by animals (such as horses) that do not become infected. Ideally, land should be left for a year before sheep are reintroduced. However, a period of six months is generally very effective and leads to significant increases in wool yield as well as to decreases in fatality.
- Destroy the secondary host, which in Britain, is mainly the snail *Limnaea truncatula*. Drainage can reduce the numbers of snails, as can chemicals which kill molluscs (**molluscicides**). Some

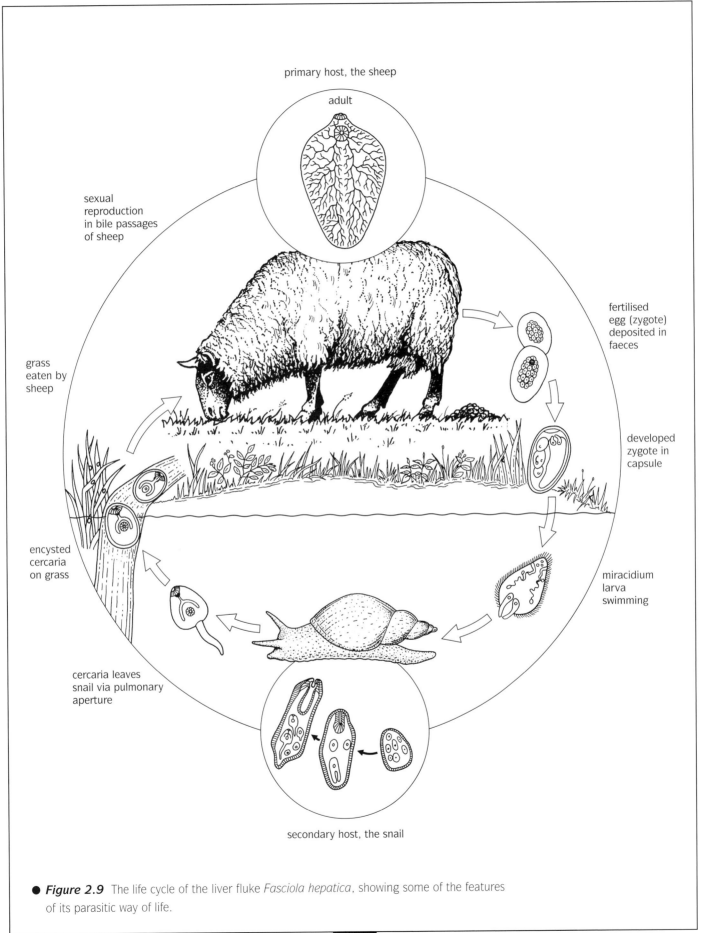

primary host, the sheep

adult

sexual
reproduction
in bile passages
of sheep

fertilised
egg (zygote)
deposited in
faeces

grass
eaten by
sheep

developed
zygote in
capsule

encysted
cercaria
on grass

miracidium
larva
swimming

cercaria leaves
snail via pulmonary
aperture

secondary host, the snail

● **Figure 2.9** The life cycle of the liver fluke *Fasciola hepatica*, showing some of the features
of its parasitic way of life.

work has been done on **biological control**. For instance, in Hawaii where *Fasciola hepatica* also occurs, a fly has been successfully introduced which has a larval stage that kills the fluke's molluscan secondary host. Introduction of new species to islands can be risky as it may upset the ecological balance, but no undesirable environmental effects have so far been reported.

- Introduce competitors of *Fasciola hepatica* that attack the same secondary hosts, the snails, but have different primary hosts that are of less economic importance (e.g. ducks). This approach is still at the research stage.
- Vaccinate sheep against liver fluke. This approach is also still at the research stage.

The association between Rhizobium and leguminous plants

While the relationship between the liver fluke and its hosts is quite one-sided, in the sense that only the liver fluke benefits, that between *Rhizobium* and its hosts is more reciprocal. Both parties benefit. Such a relationship is known as **mutualism**.

Rhizobium is the most important genus of **nitrogen-fixing bacteria**, that is, bacteria that fix gaseous nitrogen. **Nitrogen fixation** is the reduction of the nitrogen found in the atmosphere, N_2, to the ammonium ion, NH_4^+. Nitrogen-fixing bacteria are of great ecological significance as they are the only natural way, apart from lightning, in which nitrogen fixation occurs. Without nitrogen fixation, organisms would be unable to access the huge reserves of atmospheric nitrogen. Life as we know it would simply not exist as plants would be unable to make the various molecules, such as proteins and nucleic acids, that require nitrogen.

The bacteria in the genus *Rhizobium* live in the **root nodules** of many leguminous plants, including such important crop plants as peas, beans, clovers and groundnuts (peanuts). The relationship seems to benefit both the plants and the bacteria. The plants grow faster and, as we saw earlier (see page 10), they can often colonise early successional habitats that are difficult for other flowering plants because of the nutrient-poor status of the soil. The bacteria benefit by being provided with a protective home, as the root nodules reduce the likelihood of their being eaten by other organisms. In addition, the bacteria receive sugars from their hosts.

Investigations have shown that *Rhizobium* can survive in soil in the absence of host plants. Under these circumstances the bacteria feed **saprotrophically**, living off the remains of dead organisms. However, the proximity of a damaged leguminous root cell enables the bacteria to invade the legume. The plant then produces root nodules (*figure 2.10*). These root nodules are necessary for the bacteria to fix nitrogen. They contain **leghaemoglobin**. This functions rather like our own haemoglobin in that it traps oxygen. In the root nodules its role is to prevent too much oxygen from reaching the enzymes that fix the nitrogen. This is important because these enzymes fail to work if there is too much oxygen around, possibly because the nitrogen molecule (N_2) and the oxygen molecule (O_2) are similar in size and shape.

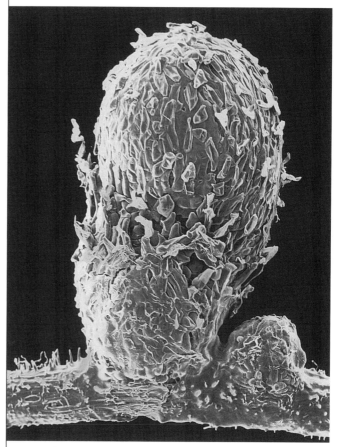

● **Figure 2.10** A scanning electron micrograph of a root nodule, caused by *Rhizobium*, on a pea plant (magnification ×16).

The enzyme responsible for nitrogen fixation is called **nitrogenase**. Plant breeders have dreamt for years of being able to breed the ability to fix nitrogen into the world's major crops, such as rice, wheat and maize. The hope has been that this would increase yields and reduce the financial and environmental costs of applying huge amounts of nitrogen-based fertilisers to the soil. With the advent of **genetic engineering** this dream has seemed attainable. It has been suggested that the gene(s) responsible for nitrogen fixation could simply be transferred from the bacteria to the crop plant, rather as the gene for insulin synthesis has been successfully transferred from humans to bacteria, allowing the manufacture by bacteria of human insulin for diabetics.

Unfortunately, there are no fewer than 17 genes responsible for the synthesis of nitrogenase! Although its chemical structure is still not completely known, nitrogenase is clearly a most complex protein. This is probably because it is very difficult to break open the nitrogen molecule. Nitrogen (N_2) is extremely stable. It is thought that as many as 16 molecules of ATP are required to fix one molecule of N_2!

It has now been discovered that many grasses, although they do not have root nodules, *do* have nitrogen-fixing bacteria associated with their roots. Most of our major crops, including wheat, rice and maize, are grasses. How important these root bacteria are for grasses is still uncertain, but their presence suggests that many more plants than just legumes may already be benefiting from nitrogen-fixing bacteria even without the aid of genetic engineering.

SUMMARY

- A population is a group of individuals from the same species that have the opportunity to breed with one another in a particular locality. Any one species is typically divided into many populations by virtue of geographical separation.

- Increases in population size can often be represented by the sigmoid growth curve.

- Limiting factors prevent populations from increasing in size indefinitely. Examples of limiting factors include food, water, space and nesting sites.

- The maximum number of individuals that an environment can sustain is known as the carrying capacity.

- Intraspecific competition occurs when individuals within a species find resources in short supply.

- Interspecific competition can be difficult to demonstrate in nature. One probable example is competition between red and grey squirrels in British woodlands.

- In northern Canada, snowshoe hare numbers go through population cycles that are still imperfectly understood. These hare cycles cause lynx numbers to cycle in synchrony.

- The general term given to a relationship between two species is symbiosis.

- The relationship between the liver fluke, its primary host (the sheep) and its secondary host (a snail) is one of parasitism. Understanding the life cycle of the liver fluke is an aid to its control.

- The association between nitrogen-fixing *Rhizobium* bacteria and leguminous plants is mutualistic.

Questions

1 Discuss the factors that limit population size in **humans** and in **one** other species.

2 Explain how the anatomical and reproductive adaptations of the liver fluke suit it for its parasitic way of life.

Chapter three

Practical ecology

By the end of this chapter you should be able to:

1 describe the use of quadrats, point quadrats and transects;

2 measure and calculate species frequency, species density and percentage cover;

3 measure the following abiotic factors in a habitat – temperature, pH, light, oxygen content, water content, mineral content;

4 assess the size of a mobile animal population using the capture–recapture technique, and explain the reasons for the assumptions made in the use of this technique;

5 outline the use of indicator species to assess the levels of air and water pollution;

6 assess the levels of air pollution (sulphur dioxide) and water pollution (organic matter) in an area, given access to appropriate identification keys.

The aims of practical ecology

We can only gain an understanding about the ecosystems (and thus biomes) around us by getting information about them through practical ecology. However, whole ecosystems are often far too complex to understand all in one go. It is easier to begin by choosing one or two species, or a small area of habitat, to study in detail. Practical ecology involves observing, taking measurements and sometimes testing ideas by experimentation.

The study of an area often includes the observation of *biological* features, such as the presence and relative abundance of the various organisms. It also involves the measurement of *physical* characteristics, such as the rainfall and temperature. Without a detailed description of the study area an ecologist will be unable to make predictions about *how* the area may change over time – whether, for example, succession will occur, or whether a particular species is at risk of dying out there.

So, in this chapter we shall look at the various techniques available to ecologists that enable them to:

■ identify the organisms present;
■ assess their relative abundance and distribution;
■ study their interrelationships;
■ measure aspects of the physical environment.

Species identification

The only ways to identify species are either to get someone who knows about them to help you, or to use an **identification key**. Identification keys come in various forms. The most widely used is the **dichotomous key**. Here successive questions are asked. 'Dichotomy' means 'division into two' and each question can be answered either 'yes' or 'no'.

An example of a dichotomous key is given in *table 3.1*. This shows the start of part of a key to over 600 species of fungi found in Britain and northern Europe. It is taken from a standard guide to these fungi. The fungi in the part of the key shown in *table 3.1* all have in common fruit-bodies that are found on wood and are bracket-shaped, irregularly lobed or crust-like. It is called 'Key F' because there are separate keys to other fungi that do not fall into this category, for instance fungi that produce fruit-bodies that are mushroom-shaped.

To use the key in *table 3.1*, you first have to decide whether the fruit-body of the fungus you are interested in is:

■ *either* bracket-shaped, ligulate or crust-like with distinctly expanded margins;
■ *or* forms a crust or is irregularly lobed and gelatinous.

If it is the former you go to question 2; if the latter, you go to question 12.

As well as demonstrating the principles behind dichotomous keys, the key in *table 3.1* illustrates two other important points about keys. First of all, they can be difficult to use! In particular, most keys

KEY F
Fruit-bodies bracket-shaped, irregularly lobed or crust-like; on wood

1. Fruit-bodies bracket-shaped, ligulate or crust-like with distinctly expanded margins, 2
1. Forming a crust, or irregularly lobed and gelatinous, 12
2. Underside with pores or gills, 3
2. Underside with teeth, tuberculate, reticulate or smooth, 7
3. Underside with round or angular pores, 4
3. Underside with greatly elongated gill-like pores, 5
4. Flesh soft, red, exuding red juice, *Fistulina* 74
4. Otherwise, Polyporaceae 62
5. Flesh bright rusty brown to yellowish brown, *Gloeophyllum* 70
5. Flesh white or dull brown, 6
6. Flesh thick, woody; on stumps especially of oak, *Daedalea* 66
6. Flesh thin, woody; upper surface ± woolly-hairy, *Trametes betulinus* 70
7. Underside smooth or tuberculate, 8
7. Underside reticulate or with teeth, 9
8. Yellow, greyish or violet; hymenium smooth, *Stereum* 50
8. Dark (reddish) brown; hymenium bristly (lens), *Hymenochaete* 52
9. Underside with teeth, 10
9. Underside (sometimes upper side) reticulately veined, 11
10. Greyish, gelatinous, *Pseudohydnum gelatinosum* 224
10. Whitish, yellow; brittle, Hydnaceae 58
11. Upper surface greyish white, silky hairy, *Merulius tremellosus* 52
11. Upper surface greyish brown, *Serpula* 52
12. Crust-like, 13
12. Ear-shaped or folded-contorted; distinctly gelatinous, 18
13. Under surface with pores; orifices sometimes jagged, Polyporaceae 62
13. Under surface smooth or tuberculate, 14
14. Hard, coal-black, 15
14. Soft-fleshed, 16
15. Large irregular, crust-like, *Ustulina* 46
15. 0.5 cm across, bursting through bark; disc-like, angular, *Diatrype* 46
16. Orange; somewhat tuberculate, *Phlebia radiata* 52
16. Whitish, greyish or brown, 17
17. Whitish, greyish or pale brown, *Corticium* 50
17. Yellowish brown with small brown warts, *Coniophora puteana* 52
18. Ear-shaped, brownish; especially on elder, *Auricularia* 224
18. Contorted; yellow, white, black or blackish-brown, *Tremella* 224

● **Table 3.1** Part of a dichotomous key to over 600 species of fungi found in Britain and northern Europe

require the user to be familiar with specialised, technical terms. A good identification key should provide you with a **glossary** to explain these technical terms.

Secondly, the key does *not* have to go all the way to individual species. Notice that this key sometimes goes to the individual species (e.g. *Trametes betulinus* (page 70) and *Pseudohydnum gelatinosum* (page 224)), but often only goes to individual genera (e.g. *Fistulina* (page 74) and

Gloeophyllum (page 70)). In some cases the key only goes as far as individual families (e.g. Polyporaceae (page 62) and Hydnaceae (page 58)).

Many people get worried about not being able to identify organisms to individual species. Yet a great deal of valuable ecology can still be done even if you cannot do this. For example, it is very difficult to identify insects to species level. However, it does not take long to be able to distinguish the 27 orders of insects found in Britain and northern Europe. These are listed in *table 3.2*. You can probably recognise half-a-dozen or more of these already. Any book on the identification of insects will provide pictures and notes to enable you to tell the others apart.

There are other types of key aside from dichotomous keys. One which is becoming more popular is the **lateral key**. Part of a lateral key to the families of British spiders is shown in *figure 3.1*. The idea is that you first look at the various features of the spider you wish to identify: size, body form, eyes, legs/claws, spinnerets (which make the silk), web and any other distinctive features. You then compare your spider with the drawings and notes shown alongside (lateral to – hence the name of the key) each of the 34 families of British spiders.

Latin name of the order	English names of insects in the order
Thysanura	silverfish and bristletails
Diplura	(tiny soil-living insects)
Protura	(minute soil-living insects)
Collembola	springtails
Ephemeroptera	mayflies
Odonata	dragonflies
Plecoptera	stoneflies
Orthoptera	crickets and grasshoppers
Phasmida	stick and leaf insects
Dermaptera	earwigs
Embioptera	web-spinners
Dictyoptera	cockroaches
Isoptera	termites
Psocoptera	booklice
Mallophaga	biting lice
Anoplura	sucking lice
Hemiptera	true bugs
Thysanoptera	thrips
Neuroptera	alder flies, snake flies and lacewings
Mecoptera	scorpion flies
Lepidoptera	butterflies and moths
Trichoptera	caddis flies
Diptera	true flies
Siphonaptera	fleas
Hymenoptera	bees, wasps and ants
Coleoptera	beetles
Strepsiptera	(parasites of bees)

● **Table 3.2** The 27 orders of insects found in Britain and northern Europe

BODY FORM	CEPHALOTHORAX & EYES	LEGS/CLAWS	SPINNERETS	DISTINCTIVE FEATURES	WEB/ECOLOGY
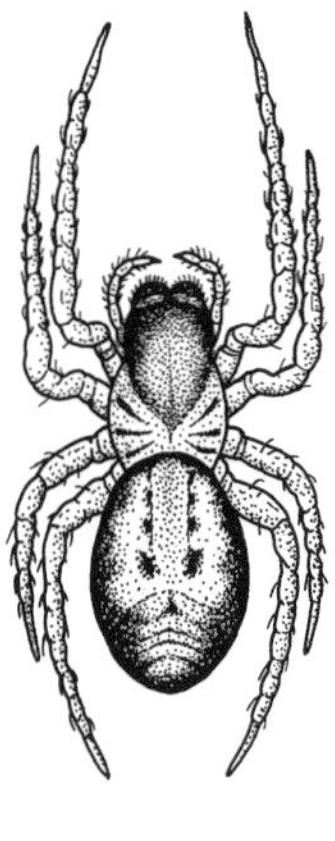	Eight eyes in two rows. Head area dark. 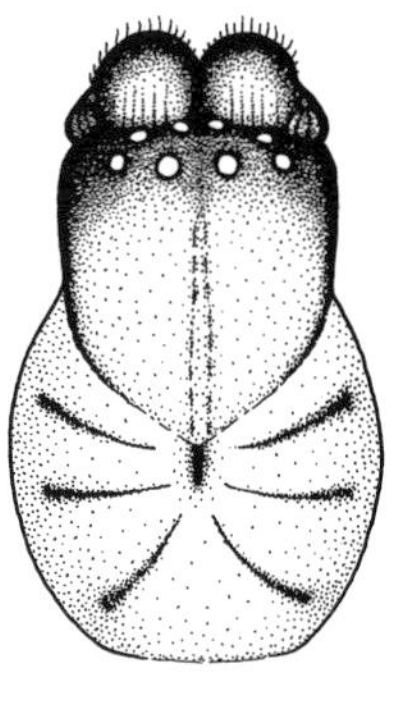	With calamistrum (c) on metatarsus IV of two rows in females. Three claws. 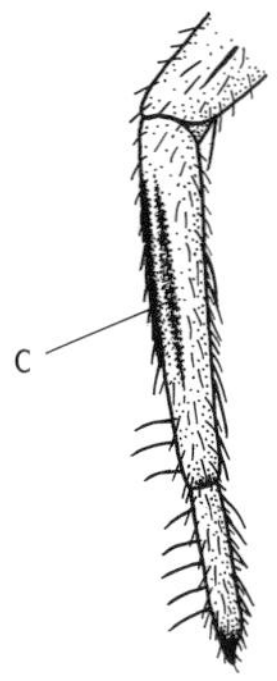	With cribellum (c). 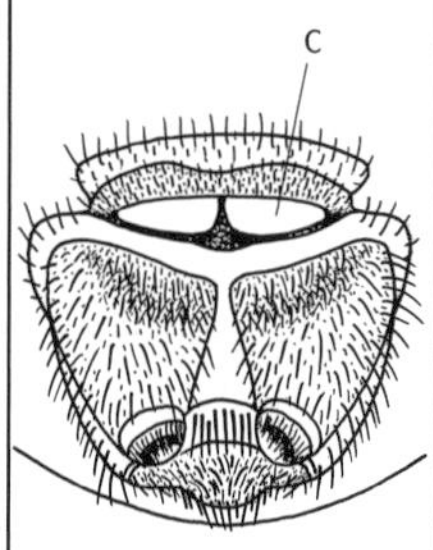	Cribellum and calamistrum. Tarsi with dorsal row of trichobothria increasing in length towards tip (t). Web in field. 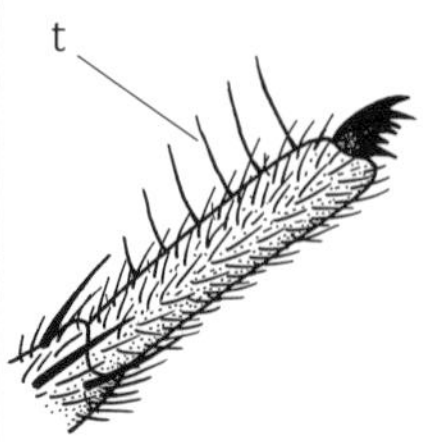	Tangled 'fuzzy' web with circular retreat in walls or tree bark. Occasionally found wandering in buildings. 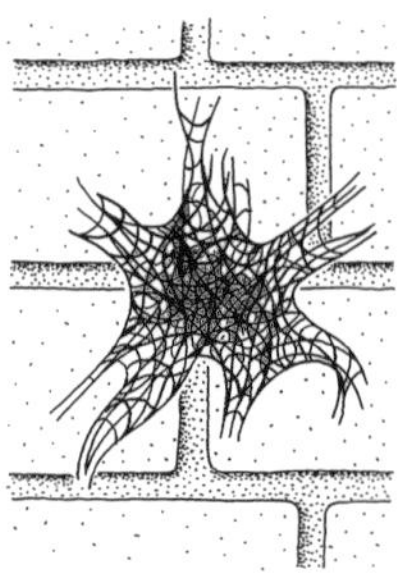

● **Figure 3.1** Part of a lateral key to the families of British spiders. This part of the key relates to the family of lace-webbed spiders, called the Amaurobiidae, which contains three species in Britain.

Determining the abundance of organisms

Once you have identified your organisms, it is often useful to know how many of them there are. Knowing this helps you to understand the relative importance of different organisms in a particular habitat or ecosystem.

In an earlier chapter we looked at how to count the number of bacteria or yeast in a population (see pages 15–16) using serial dilutions or a haemocytometer. In each case we made the assumption that the individuals in the population were spread evenly throughout the habitat. While this may be approximately true for bacteria and yeast grown in liquid cultures in the laboratory, it will rarely be the case for organisms in a natural setting.

Because of the uneven distribution of organisms in most environments, ecologists need to employ **random sampling** to determine the abundance of the organisms they are studying. In practice, random sampling is fairly straightforward. Suppose you are studying the plants in a meadow that is some 40 m long and 15 m wide. You will need a table of random numbers which lie evenly between 0 and 10, or some other device such as a computer program, to give you these numbers. (Tables of random numbers are included in most statistical tables.) Now obtain one random number between 0 and 10. Multiply it by 4 (because the meadow is 40 m long). This tells you how far to go in metres along the longer side of the meadow. Now obtain a second random number between 0 and 10 and multiply it by 1.5 (because the meadow is 15 m wide). This tells you how far to go in metres along the shorter side of the meadow. You now have two coordinates to tell you where to place a quadrat.

Quadrats

A **quadrat** is a sampling unit of known area. Quadrats are usually square frames that can be carried about and positioned with ease (*figure 3.2*). The size of the quadrat depends on the habitat and the organisms to be examined. Plant quadrats are often 0.5 m × 0.5 m. This size is ideal for grassland. Larger quadrats may be needed for heathland or

● *Figure 3.2* A 0.5 m × 0.5 m quadrat in use in species-rich grassland in central Scotland.

woodland. This is because too small a quadrat may lead, by chance, to one species (e.g. an oak tree) being over-represented or under-represented. There are no hard and fast rules but quadrats of up to 4 m × 4 m may be needed in woodland. Of course, the disadvantage with such a large quadrat is that it takes a long time to use. There is therefore a trade-off between the advantage of using a larger quadrat (more data obtained) and the disadvantage (more time taken). You could, of course, use a small quadrat to sample the ground flora of the wood and a very large one to sample the tree species.

Quadrats can be used for any sessile organisms such as plants, lichens, attached seaweeds and certain animals (e.g. barnacles). How do ecologists record the abundance of the organisms under investigation? Several approaches are used. The simplest is to use **species frequency**. Here each species is recorded as being present or absent in each quadrat. The species frequency equals the percentage of the quadrats in which the species is found. For example, suppose you examine ten quadrats in an oak woodland and find that bluebells are present in three of them. Bluebells are said to occur with a frequency of 30%. Note that this figure depends on the size of the quadrat.

SAQ 3.1

What is the effect on the species frequency of taking the same number of quadrats, but increasing the size of the quadrat used?

Quadrats can also be used to measure the **density** of species. The density of a species is the average number of individuals of that species found per unit area. So, for example, if ten 0.5 m × 0.5 m quadrats reveal a total of 140 bluebells in an oak woodland, the density is given by the equation:

$$\text{density} = \text{number of individuals} \div \text{area}$$
$$= 140 \div (10 \times 0.5\,\text{m} \times 0.5\,\text{m})$$
$$= 140 \div 2.5\,\text{m}^2$$
$$= 56\,\text{m}^{-2}$$

That is, 56 bluebells per square metre.

The major problem with using density as a measure of the abundance of some species is knowing where one individual ends and another one of the same species begins. This is not usually a problem when studying animals, but with certain plants – think of grass in a lawn – it can be impossible to decide where one individual finishes and another starts.

Because of the difficulties that can arise when using species density as a measure of abundance, another approach is to determine **percentage cover**. Here the percentage of each quadrat covered by each species is measured. The percentage can either be recorded as a number (e.g. 1% or 15%), or a scale can be used. One widely used scale is the **DAFOR scale**. Here **D** stands for dominant, **A** for abundant, **F** for frequent, **O** for occasional and **R** for rare. Obviously this scale is very subjective and

Cover/%	Braun-Blanquet scale
< 1	+
1–5	1
6–25	2
26–50	3
51–75	4
76–100	5

● **Table 3.3** The Braun-Blanquet scale used to assess the percentage cover of vegetation

it is difficult to get good agreement between different people – in other words, inter-observer reliability is low. However, it is quick and can be useful when employed by one person working alone with a large number of quadrats to assess.

A more objective scale often used when assessing the percentage cover of vegetation is provided by the **Braun-Blanquet scale**. This is explained in *table 3.3*. Whatever the precise method used to record percentage cover, the accuracy of the estimate can often be improved by subdividing the quadrat. For instance, pieces of string at 10 cm intervals can be used to divide a 0.5 m × 0.5 m quadrat into 25 smaller quadrats.

Another type of quadrat used is the **point quadrat** (*figure 3.3*). Imagine you are assessing the abundance of species of plants in a habitat by means of species frequency (i.e. the percentage of quadrats in which the species occurs). Now imagine what happens as the quadrat size gets smaller and smaller, eventually ending up as a point. In this case, placing a quadrat on the vegetation is equivalent to placing a needle, or point, on the vegetation. This is what a point quadrat is. All you need to do is to record the percentage of the needles (i.e. point quadrats) that come into contact with each species as the needle is lowered vertically. Note that it is perfectly possible for one needle to strike more than one species, so that the total of all the percentages determined by point quadrats may exceed 100%.

The capture–recapture technique

The methods of measuring species abundance we have considered so far in this chapter have been applicable only to sessile organisms. The **capture–recapture** technique, on the other hand, requires the organisms to be mobile. In this technique, also known as the **mark–release–recapture** method, the first stage is to catch a sample of individuals. Voles, for example, might be caught by a **Longworth trap** (*figure 3.4*).

Once you have caught a sample of animals, the next thing to do is to count them and then mark them in some way which causes neither harm or distress. Voles, for instance, can be marked by

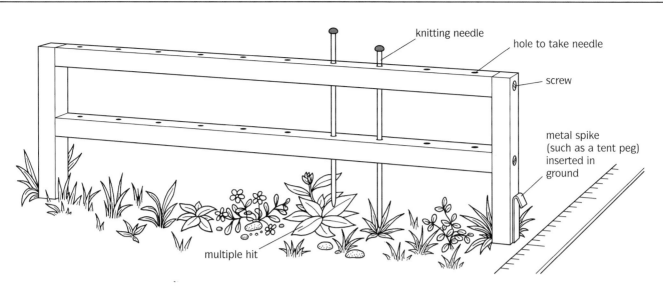

● **Figure 3.3** A home-made point quadrat frame. Two of the ten needles have been lowered.

clipping off a small piece of their fur. Whirligig beetles (to give an example of an aquatic surface insect) can be marked by putting a minute drop of waterproof paint on one of their elytra (hardened front wings).

Once the animals have been marked, they are released and allowed to mix thoroughly with the rest of the unmarked population. After a suitable period of time, a second sample is obtained and counted, and the number of marked individuals recorded. An estimate of the total size of the population can then be made. Suppose you mark 30

● **Figure 3.4** A Longworth trap, used to catch small mammals such as voles and mice.

whirligig beetles and then release them back into their original habitat – a ditch. A few hours later, once the marked individuals have mixed with the rest of the population, you catch a further 40 whirligig beetles from the same area and find that 5 of them are marked. As only 1 in 8 (i.e. 5 out of 40) of the animals you caught the second time were marked, the chances are that you only marked one-eighth of the total population. In that case, the best estimate you can make of the overall population size is 30 multiplied by 8, that is 240.

In general, the best equation for working out the size of a population by this method is called the **Lincoln index**. It is given by the formula:

$$\text{Population size} = \frac{n_1 \times n_2}{n_m}$$

So your estimate for the whirligig beetles would be

$$\frac{30 \times 40}{5} = 240$$

where n_1 is the number of individuals marked and released ('1' because it was the first sample), n_2 is the number of individuals caught the second time round ('2' because it was the second sample) and n_m is the number of marked individuals in the second sample ('m' standing for marked).

Using the Lincoln index to estimate population size involves making a number of assumptions:

■ the marked animals mix thoroughly back into the original population;

- marked and unmarked animals do not differ in any significant way – for example, marked individuals are no more likely to emigrate from the population or die than unmarked individuals;
- the marks do not wear off before the second sample is taken;
- no (or very few) births in or immigration into the population occur during the time that elapses between the two samplings.

SAQ 3.2

Predict the effect on the estimate of population size using the **Lincoln index** in each of the following circumstances.

a Insufficient time elapses before the animals are recaptured, and the second sample is taken from the same place as the first.

b Insufficient time elapses before the animals are recaptured, and the second sample is taken from a different place to the first.

c Some of the marks wear off before the second sample is taken.

d Marked animals are more likely to be caught by predators.

e Marked animals become 'trap-happy' and are more likely to be caught in traps (e.g. because traps are baited with food).

f The interval between the first and second sample is such that most of the individuals in the original population have died and been replaced by new births.

Investigating the distribution of species

The distribution of immobile species can be studied using **transects**. 'Transect' means 'cut across' and transects are of two types. A **line transect** is when a long piece of string or rope is placed on the ground and the organisms in contact with the line are identified and recorded. A **belt transect** is when a series of quadrats is placed along a line at regular intervals and the organisms in each quadrat are identified and their abundance recorded.

Transects are particularly useful when there is a clear, fairly regular change in the species of organisms found between the two ends of the transect.

For example, transects can be used to investigate the changes in vegetation as you go from grassland into neighbouring woodland, or the changes in sessile animals (such as barnacles, limpets and periwinkles) as you go up a rocky shore from the sea to the high tide zone and beyond.

Various techniques are available to study the distribution of mobile organisms. Longworth traps have already been mentioned (see page 30 and *figure 3.4*). If set out at regular intervals on a grid, these traps can be used to map the distribution of small mammals such as mice and voles. In much the same way, the distribution of ground arthropods can be studied using **pitfall traps** (*figure 3.5*). Insects and other arthropods on plants can be collected by the use of strong **nets** or **beating trays**. A **pooter** (*figure 3.6*) can then be used to collect specimens for identification, after which the organisms can be returned to their natural habitat.

Freshwater organisms can be sampled by the use of nets. Coarse nets have a mesh of about 1 mm and gather invertebrates. Finer nets can be used to sample **plankton** – small aquatic organisms that drift almost passively. A mesh size of 0.3 mm is suitable for **zooplankton** (the larvae of animals). A mesh size of 0.075 mm can be used for **phytoplankton** (e.g. microscopic algae) and protozoa (unicellular heterotrophs such as *Amoeba* and *Paramecium*).

One way of sampling freshwater invertebrates in a stream or river is by **kick sampling**. This method is particularly suitable for animals that live in or on

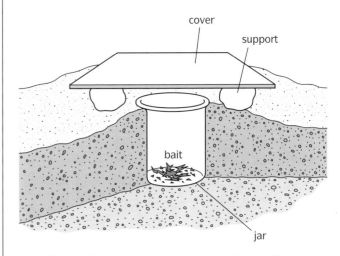

● *Figure 3.5* A pitfall trap complete with bait. The cover serves to exclude rain and certain predators.

● *Figure 3.6* A pooter being used to suck up a small arthropod so that it can be identified.

the soil that makes up the bed of a stream. A coarse net is held downstream of the area to be sampled. The bed of the stream immediately upstream of the net is then disturbed by three or four kicks directed upstream. Dislodged animals are carried into the net by the current. Although the method may sound crude, if consistently applied in different areas it can allow semi-quantitative comparisons to be made. It is advisable to wear Wellington boots.

Other sampling approaches to examine the distribution of organisms include:

■ mist nets to catch birds or bats which can then be given identification rings;

■ light traps to catch night-flying moths;
■ **Tullgren** and **Baermann funnels** to sample soil organisms *(figure 3.7)*.

Relationships between species

Interrelationships between species are of many sorts. Perhaps the most direct is where one species eats another. These sorts of relationships can be described by means of **food chains** and **food webs** which show the passage of energy and nutrients in an ecosystem. A variety of techniques can be used to obtain the data to build up food chains and food webs. Direct observation can help, as can careful analysis of stomach contents or faecal remains. More sophisticated approaches include the use of radioactive tracers or antibodies to specific antigens to trace the path of particular substances within an ecosystem.

Many other kinds of relationships can be studied by careful observation. For example, **pollination** studies may involve:

■ identification of the plant that is pollinated;
■ identification of its pollinators;
■ behavioural studies of the pollinators – how they move between plants and whether they are species-specific in their visits;
■ investigation of the rewards offered by the plant, for example the nutrient and energy value of nectar and pollen.

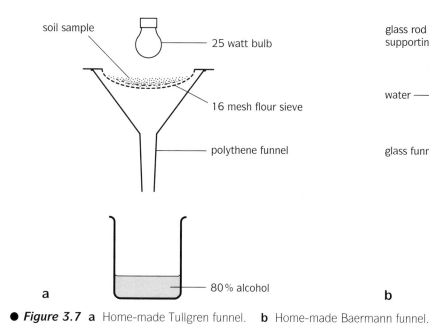

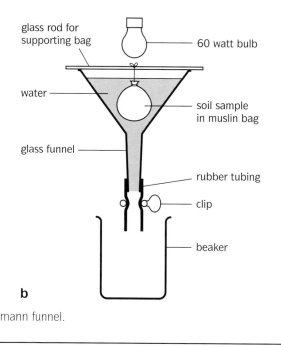

● *Figure 3.7* **a** Home-made Tullgren funnel. **b** Home-made Baermann funnel.

Measuring the physical environment

So far we have concentrated on the biological parts of ecosystems. However, much of practical ecology involves studying the physical environment. Relevant components of the physical environment (such as temperature and mineral levels) are called **abiotic factors.**

Nowadays many abiotic factors can conveniently be monitored and recorded by means of **electronic probes.** When connected to some **datalogging equipment,** such probes allow these factors to be recorded automatically at fixed intervals over varying periods of time. Such facilities are a great boon to ecologists. For instance, you could use them to record temperature, oxygen concentration and pH levels in a pond at hourly intervals over a period of 24 hours. Variations in these physical factors can then be related tentatively to variations in the physiology and behaviour of organisms, allowing testable hypotheses to be generated.

It should be remembered that many organisms, especially those living within other organisms or in the soil, live in *microhabitats.* Abiotic factors may be very different in such microhabitats from the rest of the habitat only a few millimetres away. For this reason, abiotic factors should ideally be recorded using instruments which can be positioned very precisely without affecting the microhabitat in any way. Fine, flexible probes are especially useful for this.

Temperature

For poikilothermic organisms, the ambient temperature has a significant effect on the metabolic rate and activity of the organism. Only homoiothermic birds and mammals are, to a certain extent, free from the extreme influence of temperature. Temperature is generally best measured by electronic probes, though the traditional mercury thermometer still has its uses, especially if it is a maximum and minimum thermometer. Such a thermometer displays the current temperature and records the highest and lowest temperatures experienced since it was last set.

pH

The pH of an aqueous solution is a measure of the number of H^+ ions dissolved in it. The higher the pH, the fewer the number of H^+ ions there are and, in general, the more OH^- ions. On the other hand, the lower the pH, the more H^+ ions there are and the fewer the number of OH^- ions. The pH of a habitat is important not so much because of the direct effect that H^+ or OH^- ions have on organisms, but because the pH affects the availability of other inorganic ions to organisms. For example, at a pH below about 4.5, aluminium ions, Al^{3+}, become more soluble. This is of significance as aluminium ions are toxic to many species, particularly some plants and fish.

There are many different types of pH meter, but it can be quite difficult to obtain accurate, repeatable readings. pH electrodes usually require calibration before use and should be treated carefully and in accordance with the manufacturer's instructions. Soil samples in particular may require specialised preparation before their pH can be taken.

Light levels

Light intensity and wavelength are of great importance to organisms, particularly those that photosynthesise. Specialised equipment is needed to record the **spectral composition** of light, that is the relative contribution of different wavelengths. Blue and red light are absorbed and used more than green light by chloroplasts, which is why most leaves are green in colour. Blue light, being of a shorter wavelength, penetrates water more than green or red. Because of this, many seaweeds have pigments that trap only these shorter wavelengths. As a result, such seaweeds are brown or red in colour.

Several types of **light meter** are available, but the details of their operation need not concern us. Various units are used in the measurement of **light intensity.** Perhaps the most widely used unit is watts per square metre ($W\,m^{-2}$), used to measure the total radiation falling on an area. Other instruments measure the **intensity of visible radiation** falling on an area (measured in lux) and still others measure the **intensity of photosynthetically active radiation** (also measured in lux). The important thing is to use the same instrument in the same way when taking a number of readings.

Oxygen content

In the atmosphere, oxygen concentrations vary little. However, in water and in soil, oxygen concentrations can vary a lot. It is difficult to determine the oxygen content of soil air as the sampling method tends to introduce atmospheric air. However, the oxygen content of water can be measured either by the use of probes within the natural habitat or by determining the oxygen content of a sample taken underwater so as not to introduce air bubbles.

The traditional method is the **Winkler technique**. A sample of water is obtained and the oxygen content determined by a chemical method in which Mn^{2+} is oxidised to Mn^{3+}. The amount of Mn^{3+} is then determined by titration. The Winkler method is reliable but fiddly and difficult to carry out in the field. (It requires a number of different chemical reagents including concentrated sulphuric acid.) Nowadays probes are more often used. Within the probe a current is generated the size of which depends on the dissolved oxygen content. Oxygen probes can be temperamental and careful calibration is always advisable.

Water content

Water is a prerequisite for metabolism and a major constituent of living cells. Obtaining and keeping water is thus vital for most organisms. Atmospheric humidity is an important factor in the **microclimate** affecting many organisms. **Relative humidity** is the most frequently used expression of the amount of water in the air. It equals the percentage of water vapour the air holds relative to that which it would hold if it was fully saturated. It can be measured by means of a **wet and dry bulb hygrometer** (*figure 3.8*). However, it is difficult to measure the relative humidity of microhabitats.

The **amount of water in a soil** can be determined as follows:

1 Weigh a sample of the soil ($W_{initial}$).
2 Heat the soil at $105\,°C$ until a constant weight is attained (W_{final}). 24 hours is generally long enough.

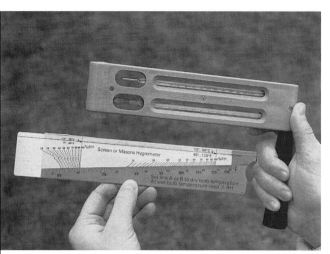

● **Figure 3.8** A wet and dry bulb hygrometer, which can be used to measure relative humidity.

3 The percentage of water in the original soil is given by

$$\% \text{ water} = \frac{W_{initial} - W_{final}}{W_{initial}} \times 100$$

Mineral content

Levels of nitrate (NO_3^-), phosphate (PO_4^{3-}), potassium (K^+) and a number of other mineral ions are of great importance to plants and other organisms in soil and water. Unfortunately, accurate measurements of most minerals are difficult, especially in soils. Various kits can be obtained from garden centres, aquarists and specialised sources, and some electronic probes are also available. Whilst the absolute levels recorded by some of the kits may be imprecise, valid comparisons between different habitats can generally be made.

Indicator species

There are basically two methods by which air and water pollution can be monitored. One is by the use of **chemical reagents** to determine the absolute levels of various pollutants, such as heavy metals and organic compounds, and high levels of nitrate (NO_3^-) and phosphate (PO_4^{3-}). The other method is the use of **indicator species**. This approach relies on observing which organisms are present and which absent from the habitat.

These two methods complement each other. Chemical reagents can be used to measure instantaneous levels of pollutants. Indicator species, on the other hand, provide a *summary* of the recent history of the environment. For example, suppose that chemical reagents reveal low levels of nitrates and phosphates while indicator species suggest high levels of these ions. The resolution of this apparent paradox might be that at some time in the recent past there was a sudden surge of nitrates and phosphates, perhaps from fertiliser or sewage run-off. The biological effects of such a surge may last a year or more even though the surge itself may be over within weeks. Nettles (*Urtica dioica*)

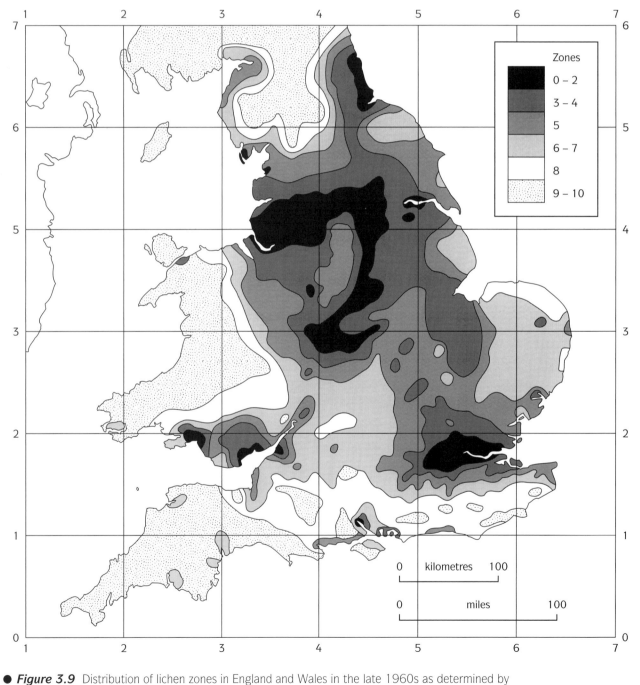

● *Figure 3.9* Distribution of lichen zones in England and Wales in the late 1960s as determined by D. L. Hawksworth and F. Rose. Zone 10 has the most species of lichens; zone 0 none.

often grow near abandoned dwellings where nutrient levels are high. The Indian balsam (*Impatiens glandulifera*) growing on stream banks can be an indicator of sewage pollution as it favours areas rich in nutrients.

Sulphur dioxide pollution of air

In a classic study in the late 1960s D. L. Hawksworth and F. Rose classified different species of lichens into ten groups, which they called zones. Zone 10 contained lichens that were particularly sensitive to atmospheric levels of sulphur dioxide (SO_2). Lichens in zone 9 could tolerate mean levels of winter SO_2 deposition of up to $30\,\mu g\,m^{-3}$. Lichens in zone 8 could tolerate levels of between 30 and $35\,\mu g\,m^{-3}$, and so on. The only lichens that could tolerate mean winter SO_2 deposition levels of $150–170\,\mu g\,m^{-3}$ were *Lecanora conizaeoides* and, less often, *L. expallens*. Zone 1 contained no lichens, only the green alga *Pleurococcus viridis*. Zone 0 contained neither lichens or algae. *Figure 3.9* shows the distribution of these lichen zones in England and Wales. As you might expect, the higher zones are found only in rural areas where the air contains the least pollutants.

Organic pollution of water

A 1980 survey of water courses in England and Wales classified streams and rivers on the basis of their dissolved oxygen concentrations, ammonia concentrations and ability to support fish. At the same time the invertebrates were categorised according to the system given in *table 3.4*. In this system, points are allocated according to whether or not **key groups** of invertebrates are present.

Families	Score
(a) Siphlonuridae, Heptageniidae, Leptophlebiidae, Ephemerellidae, Potamanthidae, Ephemeridae (mayflies) (b) Taeniopterygidae, Leuctridae, Capniidae, Perlodidae, Perlidae, Chloroperlidae (stoneflies) (c) Aphelocheiridae (beetles) (d) Phryganeidae, Molannidae, Beraeidae, Odontoceridae, Leptoceridae, Goeridae, Lepidostomatidae, Brachycentridae, Sericostomatidae (caddis-flies)	10
(a) Astacidae (crayfish) (b) Lestidae, Agriidae, Gomphidae, Cordulegasteridae, Aeshnidae, Corduliidae, Libellulidae (dragonflies) (c) Psychomyiidae, Philopotamidae (net-spinning caddis-flies)	8
(a) Caenidae (mayflies) (b) Nemouridae (stoneflies) (c) Rhyacophilidae, Polycentropodidae, Limnephilidae (net-spinning caddis-flies)	7
(a) Neritidae, Viviparidae, Ancylidae (snails) (b) Hydroptilidae (caddis-flies) (c) Unionidae (bivalve molluscs) (d) Corophiidae, Gammaridae (crustacea) (e) Platycnemididae, Coenagriidae (dragonflies)	6
(a) Mesovelidae, Hydrometridae, Gerridae, Nepidae, Naucoridae, Notonectidae, Pleidae, Corixidae (bugs) (b) Haliplidae, Hygrobiidae, Dytiscidae, Gyrinidae, Hydrophilidae, Clambidae, Helodidae, Dryopidae, Elminthidae, Crysomelidae, Curculionidae (beetles) (c) Hydropsychidae (caddis-flies) (d) Tipulidae, Simuliidae (dipteran flies) (e) Planariidae, Dendrocoelidae (triclads)	5
(a) Baetidae (mayflies) (b) Sialidae (alderfly) (c) Piscicolidae (leeches)	4
(a) Valvatidae, Hydrobiidae, Lymnaeidae, Physidae, Planorbidae, Sphaeriidae (snails, bivalves) (b) Glossiphoniidae, Hirudidae, Erpobdellidae (leeches) (c) Asellidae (crustacea)	3
(a) Chironomidae (diptera)	2
(a) Oligochaeta (whole class) (worms)	1

● **Table 3.4** The National Water Council system for monitoring organic pollution in streams and rivers. The river is given a score equal to the *highest* scored family found in the river. For example, if the river contains families which score 1, 2 and 4, then the river scores 4. The *lower* the score, the *more* polluted the river.

● *Figure 3.10* A whole range of relevant measurements can be made when working in freshwater environments. Here two students are determining the depth of a stream.

Note that the invertebrates need only be identified to family level (there are illustrated keys available to aid identification). Oligochaetes and chironomids are found even in highly polluted streams and rivers with very low levels of dissolved oxygen (<10% saturation). Low levels of dissolved oxygen result from high numbers of aerobic bacteria which use up the available oxygen as they decompose organic matter such as sewage. At the other end of the scale, most mayfly and stonefly nymphs can only survive in waters with high levels of dissolved oxygen (>80% saturation).

SUMMARY

■ Organisms can be identified by identification keys, including dichotomous and lateral keys.

■ Random sampling is generally needed to determine the abundance of organisms, due to their uneven distribution.

■ Quadrats, including point quadrats, can be used to sample sessile organisms.

■ Measures of the abundance of organisms sampled by means of quadrats include species frequency, species density and percentage cover.

■ The capture–recapture technique can be used to assess the abundance of mobile organisms provided certain assumptions hold true.

■ Transects, traps and other techniques can be used to investigate the distribution of organisms.

■ Abiotic factors, including temperature, pH, light levels and oxygen content, can often be measured by means of electronic probes and monitored by means of datalogging equipment.

■ Indicator species and chemical reagents can both be used to assess the pollution of an area.

Questions

1 With reference to **one** particular **named** habitat, discuss how its vegetation may be described.

2 Explain how **abiotic factors** are of importance in ecosystems.

3 Outline ways in which water pollution can be monitored and discuss how you could set up an investigation to record changes in the pollution of a river over time.

Chapter four

International conservation

By the end of this chapter you should be able to:

1 explain how conservation may involve preservation, management, reclamation and creation, and is a dynamic process;

2 discuss the economic and ethical reasons for maintaining biodiversity;

3 discuss the conservation of the African elephant with regard to population size, conservation measures introduced and the international cooperation required;

4 discuss the conservation of tropical rainforests with regard to their ecological importance, the reasons for their decline and the international measures that need to be, or are being, taken for their conservation;

5 discuss the causes of desertification and the remedies which may be used to combat it;

6 discuss the reasons for concern over rising levels of atmospheric carbon dioxide and the efforts being made to reverse this trend;

7 explain how chlorofluorocarbons (CFCs) damage the ozone layer and discuss the measures being taken to phase them out;

8 describe how acid rain is produced and discuss its effects on forests and lakes;

9 appreciate conflicts of interests over conservation matters.

The meaning of the term 'conservation'

At its simplest, **conservation** involves the **preservation** of endangered habitats or species. Such preservation may entail the setting-up of nature reserves or the establishment of captive breeding programmes (discussed in more detail on pages 55–6).

Often, though, conservation requires the **management** of ecosystems. Grassland, for example, usually has to be managed in some way, otherwise **succession** occurs and the grassland becomes invaded by bushes and trees. Grazing or occasional burning can help to maintain it as grassland.

A still more active form of conservation occurs when damaged habitats are restored, a process known as **reclamation**. Eroded sand dunes, for instance, may be reclaimed by the erection of sea defences or by the planting of appropriate grasses that trap blown sand, allowing it to accumulate.

The most active form of conservation involves the **creation** of new habitats. At its simplest this may be nothing more than the digging of a new pond, or the planting of a new hedge. A more ambitious scheme is currently under way in Leicestershire. Here a new national forest is gradually being planted. It should eventually cover over 450 square kilometres and include some 30 million trees, most of them broadleaved. The project is being directed by Susan Bell, a qualified planner.

The relative importance of these four conservation activities – preservation, management, reclamation and creation – varies from country to country. A few countries still have a high proportion of their land covered with its original, largely undamaged vegetation, supporting an abundance of native species. In such countries, preservation may be most important. In many countries, however, including Britain, human influence has been extensive. In such countries conservation may have to rely more on habitat reclamation and creation.

Conservation is dynamic in the sense that it is rarely sufficient simply to surround a protected area with a fence and sit back. Conservationists have to be vigilant, keeping a lookout for political and other developments, and proactive, anticipating changes in land use. Above all, successful conservation often involves reconciling conflicts between the interests of local people, governments, industry, tourists and the wildlife itself.

Why conserve?

Fundamentally there are two reasons for conservation; it can either be for the benefit of humans or for the benefit of other species.

Conservation for the benefit of humans can to some extent be described as the *economic* reason for conservation, whilst conservation for the benefit of other species can be described as the *ethical* reason for conservation.

When these two reasons for conservation come into conflict, humans generally win. Few people regret the world-wide extinction of the smallpox virus. Similarly, few people would regret the extinction of the mosquito that carries the parasite that causes malaria. What is so tragic is that often the extinction of species benefits only a few people for a brief period of time. Consider, for instance, the destruction of the tropical rainforests, a subject to which we shall return in more detail later (see pages 41–3). We know that this destruction results in the extinction of many species, that is, a loss of **biodiversity**. The gains are often short-lived and benefit only a few people – and rarely those who live in the forests. However, the long-term benefits from the preservation of tropical rainforest biodiversity are potentially huge.

Conservation of the African elephant

In the nineteenth century there were probably between 5 and 10 million African elephants, *Loxodonta africana* (figure 4.1). By 1970 there were still 3 million. By the end of 1993 there were probably just 50 000. As the biologist Colin Tudge has written of the elephant situation, 'A crisis quickly degenerates into a cliché as people lose interest, yet the crisis persists'.

Until the 1960s the elephant populations of Africa were thriving. Many elephants were shot when they encroached onto farmland and some

● **Figure 4.1** The African elephant is now an endangered species. This photograph was taken in April 1992 and shows a family group in Amboseli, Kenya.

elephants were killed for the ivory obtained from their tusks. Yet overall, numbers were healthy. In the early 1970s the price of ivory soared in response to a growing demand from Asian countries. Prices increased until by the late 1980s ivory sold for $200 to $300 a kilogram on the open market – more than the price of silver. Only some 10% of this went to the poachers, but in many African countries $300 is a good annual income.

The decline in numbers does not tell the whole tragedy. Both males and females have tusks and the animals with the largest tusks are adults. Consequently mainly adults are killed. In some areas there are no adults left. As elephants live in social groups led by mothers – elephant societies are matriarchal – young elephants now often lack the teaching and guidance that normally come from the older females: troops of young delinquent elephants can be seen aimlessly roaming the savannah. It is unclear what they will be like as parents, should they ever survive to adulthood.

In 1986 quotas for ivory export were set by the Convention on International Trade in Endangered Species of Wild Fauna and Flora (**CITES** for short). These quotas were meant to be based on what each country's elephant population was able to sustain. However, the quota system was widely abused and poaching, often using sophisticated automatic rifles, has been widespread.

In 1990 CITES responded by banning *all* international trade in tusks. As a result, the international market for ivory virtually collapsed. The price has fallen very significantly as a result and the next few years should show whether elephant numbers can begin to recover. If they do, countries with elephants will benefit from tourist income in addition to the many valuable products, including ivory, meat and elephant hide, that can be obtained directly from the animal. Tourist income from wildlife has become an important source of income for many tropical countries in recent years, and the term **ecotourism** has been coined to refer to tourism that concentrates on natural ecosystems.

Most countries have seen preservation as the way to conserve elephants. A different approach has been taken by Zimbabwe. Zimbabwe refused to support the 1990 CITES ban on the international trade in ivory. Instead it opted for a policy of management. It was argued that even in 1990 there were more elephants in Zimbabwe than the habitat could sustain. Accordingly, it set its own quotas, culled elephants and allowed ivory to be traded.

Zimbabwe's elephant policy has been part of a larger strategy aimed at managing wildlife as a valuable resource. Its CAMPFIRE programme allowed rural communities to earn money from the exploitation of wildlife. Some species are exploited for their meat, others for their hides or other products. Advocates of this programme argue that its introduction has dramatically increased the amount of land given over to wildlife – up from 12% of the country in 1988 to 35% in 1993. The reason for this increase is simply that the economic returns from wildlife have, in recent years, exceeded those from cattle.

Even if the time comes when African elephants are no longer killed for their ivory, they may still be endangered. Everywhere the growth in human population threatens their habitats. At present it is only in certain forests in the heart of Africa, such as those of the Central African Republic, that elephants seem free from human influences – so far. Even here oil prospectors are about to exploit

the area. This will threaten the unique, smaller subspecies of elephant, *Loxodonta africana cyclotis*, that these forests hold.

Before we leave the elephant we should mention that the poachers' attentions have now also turned to the Asian elephant, *Elephas maximus*. This species has long enjoyed a symbiotic relationship with humans, being almost semi-domesticated in some places. However, all Asian elephants are born in the wild, a situation which makes them vulnerable to poachers. The total numbers are now thought to have fallen to some 50 000 world-wide.

SAQ 4.1

List **five** arguments in favour of the conservation of the African elephant.

Conservation of tropical rainforests

On pages 2–3 we looked at the key features of the tropical rainforest biome. Tropical rainforests are the most diverse of all biomes. Indeed there are probably as many different species of organisms within them as there are in the whole of the rest of the world. At present tropical rainforests suffer greatly from **deforestation** – each year the Amazon rainforest loses an area the size of Belgium. Yet we know all too little about their ecology.

Currently tropical rainforests face a number of pressures.

■ They are being cut down to provide timber for export. Japan imports approximately a third of the wood exported from tropical rainforests. Once it reaches Japan, much of the wood is used for chopsticks or in the construction industry.

■ They are being cleared for the construction of roads and the building of towns, even though these are rarely wanted by the indigenous peoples. These peoples are all too often forcibly removed from their lands.

■ They are being burnt to provide land for agriculture. The main problem here is that, by and large, tropical rainforests are found on nutrient-poor soils. This is because decomposition is rapid and so most of the nutrients are found in the living organisms themselves. This means that the soils are usually unsuitable for the cultivation of agricultural crops. In Zaire, for example, the yield of cassava in the second year of cultivation on forest soil is only about 65% of the yield in the first year of cultivation. For rice the figure is 25%, and for groundnuts just 15%. The same problem occurs if the land is used for domestic herbivores, for example cattle in Amazonia to provide meat, mainly beefburgers, for the USA.

So why should we save the tropical rainforests? As always, there are ethical and economic arguments.

- Do humans have the right to cause millions of species to become extinct? After all, extinction is forever.
- Destruction of the world's tropical rainforests will contribute towards global warming, increasing the chance of disastrous changes in our climate (see page 44).
- Many drugs undoubtedly await discovery and isolation from plants found only in the rainforests.
- Rainforests can provide a sustainable crop of nuts, fruits, rubber and vegetable oils, more valuable in the long term than the short-term profits from clearing.
- Forests increase the water content of the atmosphere by transpiration. Destroying tropical rainforests decreases rainfall in the tropics.
- Deforestation often leads to **soil erosion**. Normally the dense vegetation prevents even heavy rains from washing away the soil. The plants in a rainforest act rather like a sponge, holding on to the water and only gradually releasing it into the rivers. Without the plants, floods occur and thousands of years of soil accumulation may be lost in a few weeks. Mudslides can engulf whole villages within minutes.

At the same time, it must be realised that the forces currently causing the destruction of tropical rainforests are *economic* ones. Brazil, for example, is not a wealthy country, except for the richest 10% of the population. Much of the country's foreign currency derives directly from the destruction of its forests. Opposition within Brazil to habitat destruction is often dangerous. Chico Mendes *(figure 4.2)* was a rubber tapper and the founder and spokesperson of the Union of Forest Peoples. He spoke out for the rubber tappers and Amazonian Indians, people who rely on the forest and utilise it **sustainably**. Mendes denounced those within Brazil and abroad who either cut the forests down or provide the funding for inappropriate development projects. He was shot dead in December 1988.

One ray of hope for the world's remaining tropical rainforests is that economic arguments suggest that their destruction makes financial sense only in the immediate short term. It has been calculated that after three years the accumulated profit from the sustainable exploitation of a plot within the Peruvian rainforest for rubber and fruits would exceed the profit obtained if the same plot was felled for timber.

In addition, the signing by the US government (in 1993) of the Biodiversity Treaty agreed at the 1992 Earth Summit in Rio de Janeiro is a welcome

● *Figure 4.2* Chico Mendes, a rubber tapper who fought to save the Brazilian forests and was murdered as a result.

sign. This treaty provides for countries to own the species on their land. Its ratification and implementation should ensure that countries derive a direct economic benefit from the exploitation of their natural resources by other countries and multinationals. For instance, it may be possible for tropical countries to charge royalties on medicinal products derived from their plants.

Finally, we should note that while some industrialised countries demand that tropical countries implement policies that will lead to the sustainable use of their forests, the same countries refuse to be bound by such policies themselves. In Helsinki in June 1993, European governments, led by the UK, declined to commit themselves to such sustainable forest exploitation. As a result this meeting, attended by 51 countries, ended in stalemate although the majority of the countries there (including the USA and major tropical timber producers such as Indonesia and Malaysia) were prepared to sign. This is despite the fact that Britain is one of the least wooded countries in the world. Only 8% of Britain is covered by trees, and the great majority of our forests have been planted for timber, frequently with non-native species.

In 1993, the Forest Stewardship Council was launched. This has organised the first international system for labelling tropical timber that has been sustainably produced. Its main principles are:

■ There must be a written forest management plan.
■ The impact on wildlife, biodiversity and water resources should be minimal.
■ Ownership of the forest must be clearly defined and traditional rights of indigenous people protected.
■ Profits should be shared fairly.
■ Harvesting rates of all forest products must be sustainable in the long term.
■ Plantations should not replace natural forest.

Desertification

As we saw on pages 3–5, deserts are usually characterised by an annual rainfall of less than 50 mm.

(By comparison, different parts of Britain receive between 600 and 3000 mm of rain a year.) The term **desertification** is used to refer to the spread of deserts into semi-arid lands.

Most ecologists agree that desertification results from one or both of the following causes:

■ excessive demands made on the environment by people;
■ adverse weather conditions.

Until recently it was generally supposed that the former of these causes was the more important. The argument goes as follows:

■ An increase in the number of people leads to **overgrazing** by domestic animals such as sheep or goats, or to a decrease in the number of trees as these are cut down for firewood.
■ Overgrazing and/or the loss of trees leads to a loss of vegetation and a sharp increase in soil erosion, whether by winds or occasional floods.
■ Soil erosion leads to greater demands being made on the productive land that is left.
■ As a result, the carrying capacity of the environment is grossly exceeded and the fragile soils of semi-arid regions are destroyed.
■ Starvation ensues or people migrate to neighbouring semi-arid regions, causing them, in turn, to become desert.

In addition to a growth in human population size, other human activities are also believed to lead to desertification. For example, a shift to a settled lifestyle by previously nomadic peoples can put too much local stress on a fragile environment. Even the provision of water holes can result in desertification as domestic animals destroy the vegetation around them by their frequent trampling.

Recently, however, some ecologists have become more sceptical about the extent to which human activity can cause desertification. It has been suggested, for example, that the apparent spread south by the Sahara in the 1960s and 1970s may simply have resulted from a decrease in the rainfall. The extent to which human activities can change the climate is an issue we shall return to later (pages 44–6).

Can desertification be reversed?

Historical records show that deserts wax and wane in size. However, humans have the power to influence these changes. The Kenyan Green Belt Movement has shown how beneficial tree planting in semi-arid areas can be. This project started in the early 1970s and has largely been managed by Professor Wangari Maathai. She has worked with the traditional wood-gatherers of Kenya, women who know from bitter experience the problems caused by a lack of trees. In all, some 600 tree nurseries have been established and over 7 million trees planted. Such trees provide wood for fuel, and foliage for cattle. In addition, they help prevent soil erosion.

A dramatic example of the reversal of desertification is in the Negev Desert of Israel. This scheme has been so successful that Israel is now renowned for the quality of its exported fruits. Similar schemes exist in Spain and in parts of the USA. Such projects rely on a high level of technology. It should be noted that some attempts to increase the agricultural productivity of deserts or semi-arid regions have gone disastrously wrong. One problem has been an increase in salinity of the soil as a result of the large amounts of water used in irrigation. As this water evaporates, minerals are drawn up into the surface soil from deep down. Soils can become so salty that crops are unable to grow.

Global warming

Carbon dioxide (CO_2) is an odourless, invisible gas that is vital for photosynthesis and occurs in the atmosphere at a concentration of less than 0.05%. Yet it may turn out to be the most serious pollutant of the next 50 years. Why?

The problem with carbon dioxide is that it is a major contributor to the **greenhouse effect** *(figure 4.3)*. The greenhouse effect is so called because carbon dioxide and certain other atmospheric gases warm the Earth in much the same way that glass warms a greenhouse. Light rays from the Sun that have been reflected from the Earth's surface are trapped in the atmosphere by carbon dioxide, water vapour, hydrocarbons, nitrogen dioxide and

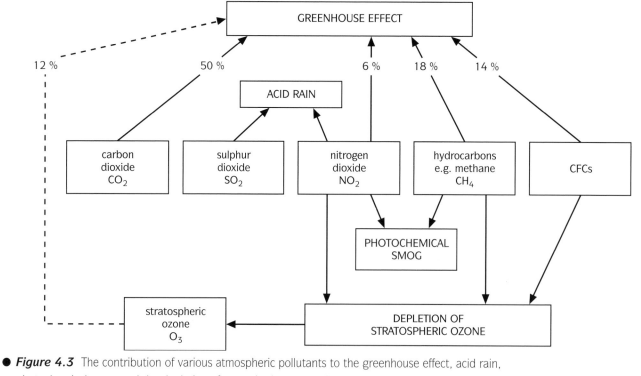

● **Figure 4.3** The contribution of various atmospheric pollutants to the greenhouse effect, acid rain, photochemical smog and the depletion of ozone in the stratosphere. Note that natural stratospheric ozone contributes to 12% of the greenhouse effect. The remaining 88% is the result of raised levels of CO_2, NO_2, CH_4 and chlorofluorocarbons (CFCs), as shown.

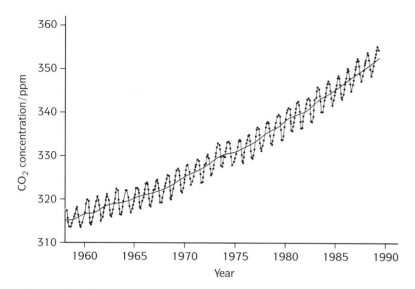

● **Figure 4.4** The atmospheric concentration of CO_2 in parts per million (ppm) measured at monthly intervals over the last 30 years. The readings were taken in Hawaii.

chlorofluorocarbons. These gases prevent heat energy escaping from the Earth's atmosphere, rather as glass prevents heat energy escaping from a greenhouse.

Measurements of the carbon dioxide concentration of air bubbles trapped in the ice of Antarctica have been made. These suggest that from about 2500 years ago up to about 200 years ago the concentration of carbon dioxide in the atmosphere was fairly constant, at around 270 parts per million (ppm). Since then, though, the atmospheric concentration of carbon dioxide has been rising at an ever-increasing rate. It has now reached over 350 ppm *(figure 4.4)*.

There are two reasons for this increase. One is that we are burning large amounts of coal, oil, gas and peat. These fossil fuels

have been laid down over hundreds of millions of years and act as **sinks** in the carbon cycle. Normally carbon, once trapped in these sinks, would rarely if ever escape. The second reason for the increase in the amount of carbon dioxide in the atmosphere is the destruction of the world's forests. Such deforestation removes trees that would otherwise act as carbon reservoirs. Methane (produced in rubbish dumps, swamps and ruminants) is another, even more effective, greenhouse gas but its build-up in the atmosphere is much less than that of carbon dioxide.

The consequences of global warming are still uncertain. We know that during the last hundred years average world temperatures have risen by over 0.5 °C *(figure 4.5)*. However, climate is very variable so we cannot be certain that the warming is due to the greenhouse effect. It is even more difficult to predict what will happen next as features such as increased cloud cover could counteract the warming. However, it is hard to see the high carbon dioxide concentrations being reversed in the near future. Attempts to model the greenhouse effect over the next 50 years suggest increases in average world temperatures of between 1 and 5 °C.

What would be the consequences of such warming? Again, we simply do not know for sure. What seems to have happened *already* is that the surface waters of the oceans at the equator have become warmer. As a result, more water is evaporating into the air.

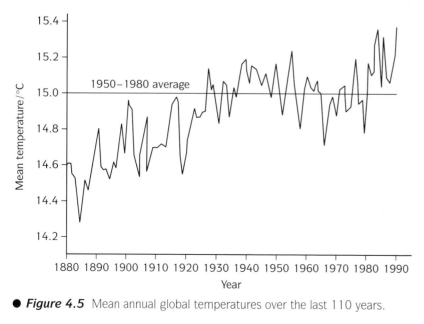

● **Figure 4.5** Mean annual global temperatures over the last 110 years.

The warmer air rises faster than usual, which results in stronger winds. These winds carry the moisture-laden air further from the tropics. Because of this, the tropics receive *less* rain than usual, whereas in temperate regions floods are *more* likely. This may be why, over the last 20 years, we seem to have had more droughts than usual in the tropics, and more extremes of weather generally.

Looking further ahead is even more difficult. To repeat, we still don't know for certain that global warming is occurring as a result of the greenhouse effect. In addition to even more unsettled weather, with consequent deaths and destruction from hurricanes and floods, the greenhouse effect might result in the melting of much of the ice caps. The resulting rise in sea levels could cause hundreds of millions of people in low-lying areas to abandon their homes.

The melting of the ice caps and a warmer climate would have profound consequences for other species. As one person put it, 'Can polar bears tread water?' The British charity Plantlife has carried out a detailed assessment of the likely effects of global warming on the British flora. Some plants would benefit. Several of our rarest and most beautiful orchids, for example, would probably increase in range. On the other hand, many plants adapted to colder conditions would probably suffer. Some of the likely consequences are surprising. Bluebells, for example, rely on cool spring weather. This allows them to grow before other, larger plants come into leaf. Warmer springs might lead to the loss of bluebells from Britain.

If levels of atmospheric carbon dioxide are to be reduced, international cooperation will be essential. A number of approaches have been suggested.

- Less reliance on fossil fuels and more on renewable ones, such as solar power and wind power, or on nuclear energy. France, for example, reduced its carbon dioxide emissions during the 1980s by making a major shift in electricity generation towards nuclear power and away from fossil fuels.
- The introduction of more energy-saving measures. The potential of this approach is often underestimated. If Britain's houses had the insulation of their Scandinavian counterparts, domestic heating bills would fall by a third.
- More trees could be planted, allowing carbon dioxide to be locked away in wood.
- People could stop expecting their standard of living to go on rising. Almost every piece of technology we buy, including cars and televisions, requires large amounts of energy in its manufacture.
- More speculative proposed solutions include pumping carbon dioxide underground or down to the ocean floor, and even encouraging massive oceanic algal blooms to trap carbon dioxide in their organic matter.

What is needed is political willpower. The Climate Change Convention, agreed at the 1992 Earth Summit, requires rich nations to halt their rising emissions of carbon dioxide. Carbon dioxide emissions *can* be cut. Britain's peaked in 1973, just before the 1974 oil crisis, when they were equivalent to 178 million tonnes of carbon a year. In 1992 they were 156 million tonnes. In 1993 Germany announced proposals to cut its emissions of the major greenhouse gases to half their 1987 levels by the year 2005. This includes a cut in the emission of carbon dioxide of 25–30%.

SAQ 4.2

The amount of carbon in the atmosphere is currently increasing at an annual rate of about 3×10^{15} g. Approximately how much is this per person alive in the world today?

SAQ 4.3

Carbon dioxide output in Britain is mainly due to burning fossil fuel in power stations and cars. Give **five** ways in which people could be encouraged to use less fossil fuel.

Destruction of the ozone layer

Ozone (O_3) is found at low concentrations 15–50 km above the Earth's surface, in the stratosphere. Here, conveniently for humans and other organisms, it intercepts much of the ultraviolet radiation that would otherwise reach the Earth's surface from the Sun. Ultraviolet radiation damages the DNA (deoxyribonucleic acid) in cells.

During the late 1980s measurements above Antarctica showed a significant decrease in the amount of ozone there. More recently, the same phenomenon has been observed above the Arctic. There are seasonal holes in the ozone layer and each year the holes are larger.

The main chemicals responsible for this thinning of the ozone layer are **CFCs (chlorofluorocarbons)** *(figure 4.6)*. Sunlight can break down CFCs to give 'free radical' (highly reactive) chlorine atoms. The problem is worst during the polar winters because at very low temperatures many more chlorine atoms are released. The chlorine atoms then react with ozone thus:

$$Cl\cdot + O_3 \longrightarrow ClO\cdot + O_2$$

The ClO· then reacts with other atmospheric components. In the stratosphere this is usually an oxygen atom:

$$ClO\cdot + O \longrightarrow Cl\cdot + O_2$$

The 'dots' after Cl and ClO indicate that they are 'free radicals'. Note that a molecule of ozone is destroyed *without* the chlorine atom being used up. It has been calculated that a single CFC molecule can remove hundreds of thousands of ozone molecules.

In the 1970s and 1980s CFCs were widely used in refrigerators, aerosol sprays and fast-food packaging. Pressure by environmentalists and scientists led to the signing (in 1987) of the **Montreal Protocol** by over 30 countries. This laid down targets to ensure that fewer CFCs were released into the atmosphere. Although some governments were reluctant to comply, there has been a significant reduction in the use of CFCs. What is still unknown is when, or even if, the holes in the ozone layer will start to shrink. Unfortunately it is known that CFCs can persist for many decades.

If the measures to protect the ozone layer fail, the most immediate probable consequence will be a significant increase in the number of cases of skin cancer. The first countries to suffer will be those, such as Australia, that are close to Antarctica. The ultraviolet rays can also damage eyes; some sheep in Australia have already gone blind.

Acid rain

Acid rain is the collective name given to a number of processes all of which involve the deposition of acidic gases from the atmosphere *(figure 4.7)*. Most deposition is indeed in acidic rain, though some direct, so-called **dry deposition**, occurs without rainwater acting as a vehicle.

Natural, unpolluted rain has a pH of about 5.6, due to the presence of dissolved carbon dioxide. However, in Britain, the rest of Europe and North America rainwater often has a pH of between 4 and 4.5 and sometimes much lower than this. A rainstorm at Pitlochry in Scotland on 10 April 1974 had a pH of 2.4 – more acidic than vinegar! This increased acidity is due to the presence of various

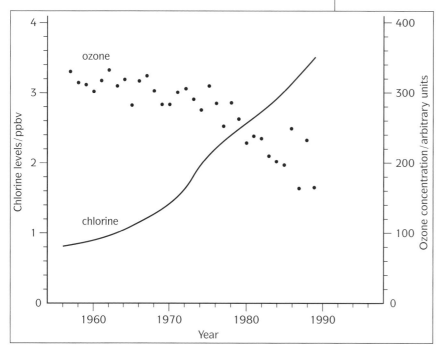

● **Figure 4.6** Changes in global average concentration of chlorine in the troposphere in parts per billion by volume (ppbv) held by halocarbons including CFCs (line) and in the total ozone over Antarctica in October (dots).

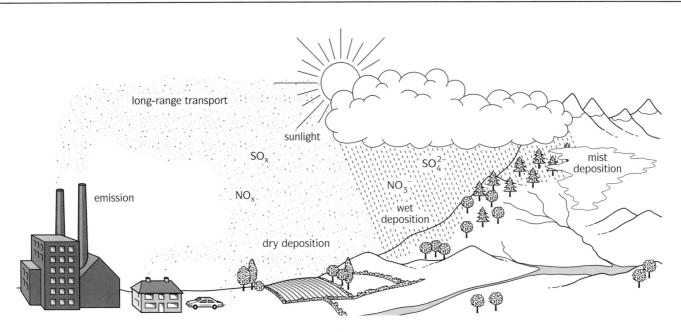

● **Figure 4.7** The transport and deposition of acid rain. The main gases involved are sulphur dioxide (SO_2) and various oxides of nitrogen (NO_x). Dry deposition occurs in the absence of rain. Wet deposition is particularly important in areas covered with mists for long periods of time.

oxides of nitrogen and sulphur, often collectively described as NO_x and SO_x. Nitrogen oxides can give rise to nitric acid and sulphur oxides to sulphuric acid.

Acid rain does not respect international borders. Just 8% of the sulphate falling on Norway comes from Norway. The other 92% comes from other countries – indeed, 17% of it comes from Britain. On the other hand, the prevailing westerly winds across Britain mean that none of the UK's sulphate deposition comes from Norway. The great majority of our sulphate deposition, 79%, is of British origin.

Acid rain results directly from the combustion of fossil fuels in power stations (coal, oil or gas) or in vehicles (petrol). Not all these sources are equally to blame. Coals with a high sulphur content are particularly harmful.

The ecological importance of acid rain is still uncertain. Many environmentalists and a large number of independent ecologists blame acid rain for much of the damage done to trees in European and North American forests. Scientists employed by the power generation industry are generally more cautious in their conclusions. The most noticeable early symptom of acid rain in trees is crown die-back, in which the top of the tree dies first. In some countries, particularly at high altitudes and at the edges of forests, large areas are covered with dead or dying trees *(figure 4.8)*.

As we saw earlier (page 37), many lichens cannot tolerate high SO_2 levels. Both trees and lichens live for a long time, which may explain their susceptibility. Among trees, conifers seem particularly at risk and, of course, most conifers are evergreen. This means that their leaves are renewed only after three or four years of exposure to the atmosphere, rather than after eight months or so as is typical with deciduous species.

● **Figure 4.8** Conifers damaged and killed by acid rain on the Czech–German border.

Acid rain also has a significant effect on fresh-water ecosystems. During the 1960s and 1970s many Scandinavian lakes lost large numbers of their fish. There are good data to show that this correlated with increasing acidification of the lakes. More recently the same problem has occurred in some Scottish lochs. The situation is most severe in lakes that lie on granite rocks. Freshwater on limestone is much better at buffering the acid.

Acid rain not only kills fish. It also interferes with the uptake of calcium by crustaceans. Without calcium, they cannot manufacture their exoskeleton. Acid rain has also been implicated in the failure of a number of bird species in the Netherlands to breed with their usual success.

The direct cause of these harmful effects is probably not the hydrogen ions (H^+) themselves. What happens is that at a low pH more aluminium (present in soil clay) can exist in solution. Aluminium is known to be toxic to many species, and some plant and fish species are particularly susceptible.

How can the problems of acid rain be reversed? The knowledge is there and the technology is there, but the measures are expensive and too many governments lack the political willpower necessary. Sadly, saving Norwegian fish stocks gains few votes at a British parliamentary or local election.

Some success has been achieved at raising the pH of a few lakes by adding large amounts of calcium carbonate (limestone). However, the only long-term solution is to reduce emissions of sulphur and nitrogen oxides. Sulphur dioxide emissions from power stations can be reduced by the introduction of sulphur dioxide scrubbers. Unfortunately, these require very large amounts of limestone. This is both expensive and requires extensive quarrying, which itself damages the environment. The British power industry is currently shifting towards the use of natural gas and imported low-sulphur coal, which should help, though at the expense of further job losses in the British coal mining industry.

SUMMARY

- Conservation may involve the preservation, management, reclamation or creation of ecosystems.

- Arguments in favour of conservation and the preservation of biodiversity may be economic or ethical.

- The total number of African elephants at the end of 1993 was 50 000, just 2 % of the total 25 years earlier. Elephants are killed mainly for ivory. Trade in ivory has now been banned by CITES.

- Tropical rainforests are being cut down for a number of reasons. Their preservation will require inter-national cooperation.

- The causes of desertification are uncertain. It occurs either because of excessive demands being made on the environment by people or because of adverse weather conditions. Desertification can be reversed

- Global warming is probably a result of the build-up of a number of atmospheric gases, the most important of which is carbon dioxide. Reducing the atmospheric level of carbon dioxide is feasible, but will not be easy.

- Chlorofluorocarbons (CFCs) are responsible for damage to the protective ozone layer. The Montreal Protocol has set limits on the use of CFCs.

- Acid rain, including dry deposition, results from the burning of fossil fuels, particularly those with a high sulphur content. Its ecological importance is still under debate. Acid rain has almost certainly damaged many freshwater ecosystems, and probably large areas of forest.

- There are nearly always conflicts of interest over conservation matters. Conservation is political.

Questions

1 Explain why tropical rainforests are being lost at such a high rate, despite the arguments for their conservation.

2 Discuss whether conservationists should concentrate on endangered species or threatened ecosystems.

3 Compare pollution caused by acid rain with that from CFCs. Suggest why an inter-national agreement exists with regard to CFCs (the Montreal Protocol) but not acid rain.

Chapter five

National conservation

By the end of this chapter you should be able to:

1 explain the role of UK government organisations in protecting ecologically important areas, with reference to National Parks, National Nature Reserves, Sites of Special Scientific Interest and Environmentally Sensitive Areas;

2 describe the role of voluntary bodies in protecting ecologically important areas in the UK, with particular reference to the Royal Society for the Protection of Birds and the Woodland Trust;

3 discuss the role of zoos with regard to captive breeding and release programmes, and the role of botanic gardens in the preservation of seed banks;

4 discuss the impact of the agricultural practices of pesticide use, hedgerow removal and drainage on conservation;

5 discuss the causes of soil erosion and the methods used to combat it.

In this chapter we look at **national** conservation. Of the world's 207 countries we shall concentrate on the United Kingdom. However, it should not be thought that the UK is fundamentally different from other countries with regard to the difficulties faced by its ecosystems. The root of the problem throughout the world is human activity. The next fifty years should show whether wildlife in the UK will exist only in isolated nature reserves scattered around the country, or whether everyone will be able to enjoy the sights and sounds of organisms in their natural habitats within walking distance of where they live.

The UK government and conservation

There are a number of different pieces of legislation in the UK giving protection to wildlife. However, as we shall see, much of the legislation has exemptions and can legally be by-passed under certain circumstances. For many people, these features gravely weaken the **statutory protection** (i.e. protection in the eyes of the law) afforded to wildlife. Existing legislation falls into two categories. One category is concerned with the preservation of important *habitats*; the other with the preservation of particular *species*. In chapter 4 we saw how conservation involves preservation, management, reclamation *and* habitat creation. However, existing UK legislation addresses only one of these four areas: preservation.

National Parks

In the UK a **National Park** is an area in England or Wales of substantial size and outstandingly attractive scenery that is specially protected and reserved for public enjoyment. Other countries have had National Parks for over a hundred years. For instance, one of the best known, Yellowstone Park in Wyoming, USA, was established in 1872. However, none existed in the UK before 1949. Their establishment was heralded in that year by the passing of the

● *Figure 5.1* Lathkilldale in the Peak National Park, the first National Park in England or Wales.

National Parks and Access to the Countryside Act. This Act went through the Houses of Parliament in a spirit of post-Second World War optimism and hope for the future.

A National Park was defined in 1945 as:

an extensive area of beautiful and relatively wild country in which, for the nation's benefit and by appropriate national decision and action:

- *the characteristic landscape beauty is strictly preserved;*
- *access and facilities for public open-air enjoyment are amply provided;*
- *wildlife and buildings and places of architectural and historical interest are suitably protected; while*
- *established farming use is effectively maintained.*

The first of the National Parks was the Peak National Park. It was soon followed by nine others, giving ten in all. These ten are shown in *figure 5.2*. The Norfolk Broads and the New Forest are also shown. Although not technically National Parks, they enjoy a very similar status. Between them the ten National Parks have a total area of 13 745 km², 8 % of the area of England and Wales. No new National Parks have been announced since 1957, though there is hope that the South Downs may soon be designated as one.

The National Parks of England and Wales are of vital importance. Nevertheless, their main function is not really the conservation of *natural eco-systems*. For a start, the landscape of England and Wales is so affected by human activity that almost no 'natural' ecosystem of any size remains. Then there is the fact that legislation permits farming, forestry and quarrying to take place in them, so that human activity is not excluded from our National Parks.

Scotland and Northern Ireland do not have National Parks. Instead, Scotland has **Regional Parks**, while Northern Ireland has **Areas of Outstanding Natural Beauty**. Both of these are essentially the same as National Parks.

National Nature Reserves

National Nature Reserves (NNRs) are smaller and more numerous than National Parks. As of January 1994 there were 268 NNRs in England, Scotland and Wales. They are identified specifically because of their importance in protecting biological diversity in Britain. However, the definitive account of the functions of National Nature Reserves in Britain, published in 1977 by the then Nature Conservancy Council, identified four functions for them *in addition* to conservation:

- research;
- demonstration and advice;
- education;
- amenity and access.

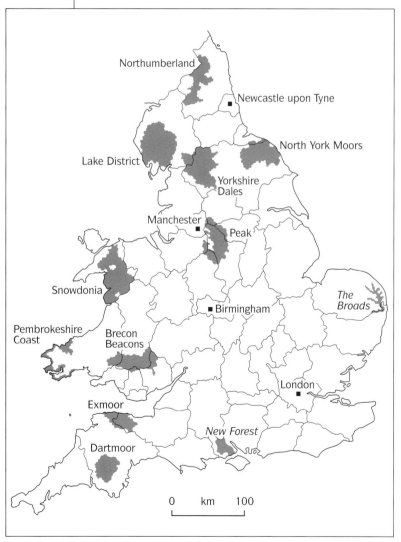

● *Figure 5.2* The ten National Parks and two equivalent areas (the Broads and New Forest) in England and Wales.

These four functions need not conflict with conservation. Indeed, given a sympathetic landowner and intelligent management, they can support and enhance conservation. However, landowners can change and not all are sympathetic to conservation. So although National Nature Reserves benefit from very strong protection under the law, they do not enjoy a guaranteed and protected future.

Sites of Special Scientific Interest

Sites of Special Scientific Interest (SSSIs), as their name suggests, are areas of particular scientific importance or note. Most are important for their existing organisms, but many are geological SSSIs, and contain rich collections of fossils that need protection. The formal definition of an SSSI is that it is 'an area of land which is of special interest by reason of its flora, fauna, geological or physiographic features'. There are about 6000 SSSIs in England, Scotland and Wales. In England their notification is the responsibility of English Nature; in Scotland it is the responsibility of Scottish Natural Heritage; in Wales it is the responsibility of the Countryside Council for Wales. A summary of the number of National Nature Reserves and Sites of Special Scientific Interest in England, Scotland and Wales is given in *table 5.1*. Northern Ireland does not have SSSIs, having instead its own **Areas of Special Scientific Interest**.

	NNRs	*SSSIs*
England	148	3749
Scotland	71	1364
Wales	49	881
Total	268	5994

● *Table 5.1* The number of National Nature Reserves (NNRs), in January 1994, and Sites of Special Scientific Interest (SSSIs), in October 1993, in England, Scotland and Wales

The important feature of SSSIs is that local planning authorities and landowners or occupiers must be informed of activities which might damage the site. In theory this should protect them from development. In practice, however, development for roads, housing or leisure amenities all too often takes place. Fully 5% of SSSIs are damaged each year. Some government money is available to help protect SSSIs, but almost no central funding exists to finance their management.

Environmentally Sensitive Areas

In 1987 the category of **Environmentally Sensitive Area (ESA)** was introduced. Such areas are determined by the Minister of Agriculture in fulfilment of the following criteria.

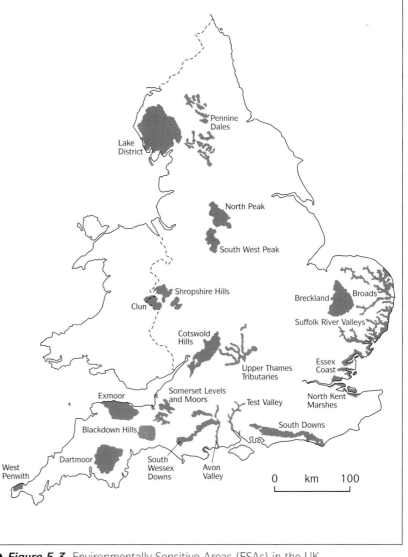

● *Figure 5.3* Environmentally Sensitive Areas (ESAs) in the UK.

Areas of national environmental significance whose conservation depends on the adoption, maintenance or extension of a particular form of farming practice; in which there have occurred, or there is a likelihood of, changes in farming practices which pose a major threat to the environment; which represent a discrete and coherent unit of environmental interest; and which would permit the economic administration of appropriate conservation aids.

At present there are a total of 22 ESAs in England and Wales *(figure 5.3)*. Farmers are paid to manage their land in ways which conserve features created by traditional land-use management. For example, some farmers are paid to keep sheep when this would otherwise be unprofitable for them. Sheep grazing preserves grassland. Chalk grasslands, in particular, are often rich in beautiful plants. Other farmers are paid not to drain their land, thus enabling water meadows and other semi-aquatic habitats to be retained.

Other UK legislation protecting wildlife

Recent years have seen a significant increase in government legislation to protect threatened habitats or endangered species. The following schemes or pieces of legislation were all introduced in the 1980s or early 1990s.

- **Nitrate Sensitive Areas** – areas where the use of fertilisers, slurry and manure is restricted and nitrate-absorbing crops are encouraged.
- **Heritage Coasts** – undeveloped coastline defined by the Countryside Commission and specified in local authority structure plans.
- **Farm Woodland Scheme** – a European Union (EU) scheme in which financial incentives are provided to encourage landowners to plant trees.
- **Set-aside** – an EU scheme in which grants are made to farmers to take at least 20% of their land out of arable production and leave the fields uncultivated.
- **The Wildlife and Countryside Act** (1981) – which protects a number of animal and plant species and their immediate habitats.
- **The Protection of Badgers Act** (1992) – which provides considerable (but not total) protection to badgers and their setts.

- **Tree Preservation Orders** – which can be put on important or mature trees by local planning authorities to protect them from being felled or damaged.

UK voluntary bodies and conservation

The UK, in common with many other countries, has a large number of **voluntary bodies**, also known as **non-government organisations** (**NGOs**), involved in conservation. Such voluntary bodies play a vital role in conservation, harnessing the enthusiasm and talent of millions of people. In addition to owning and managing land for the benefit of nature, they also act as pressure groups helping to prevent still further damage to the environment. Their income comes from membership subscriptions, company sponsorships, appeals, legacies and the sale of goods. They also often qualify for grants from local authorities or government sources.

Some of these voluntary bodies, such as the **National Trust**, have aims wider than nature conservation. The National Trust, for instance, also owns and conserves a large number of buildings. We shall look at two voluntary organisations – both of which are charities – that concentrate on nature conservation. One was formed towards the end of the nineteenth century and devotes its efforts to a particular group of organisms; the other was formed more recently and concentrates on a particular habitat.

The Royal Society for the Protection of Birds

The **Royal Society for the Protection of Birds** (RSPB) was founded in 1889 to outlaw the practice of decorating ladies' dresses and hats with birds' feathers. By 1993 it had grown into an organisation with 870 000 members and an annual turnover of £27 million.

One aim of the RSPB has been to purchase and manage nature reserves for the benefit of birds, and therefore other organisms. It owns over 120 reserves covering some 78 000 hectares. Many of these are stunningly beautiful and the visitor is almost guaranteed views of rare birds such as avocets, ospreys, marsh harriers, Dartford warblers or choughs.

In addition to its purchase and management of reserves, the RSPB is engaged in many other activities including:

fund raising, helped by an attractive quarterly journal and effective advertising *(figure 5.4)*;

prosecution of egg collectors and people who poison birds of prey;

lobbying members of parliament on conservation and farming issues;

fighting development proposals that threaten endangered habitats;

campaigning against such things as commercial peat extraction and the trade in wild birds;

researching, both in this country and overseas, into the survival and reproduction of birds which live in or visit Britain;

educating through environmental education publications and the activities of its **Young Ornithologists' Club** – for example a newsletter called *Sixth Sense* aimed at 16- to 19-year-olds is sent to all schools each term.

The RSPB can be contacted at The Lodge, Sandy, Bedfordshire, SG19 2DL, UK (tel. 01767 680551).

The Woodland Trust

The **Woodland Trust** was founded in 1972 by Kenneth Watkins because he saw the need for an organisation to acquire and manage smaller broadleaved woods. It soon became one of Britain's fastest-growing conservation groups. Its stated aim is 'to safeguard trees, small areas as well as large, by raising money to buy and look after woods that might otherwise be destroyed and to plant trees to create new woods'.

There are only this many breeding male bitterns alive in Britain today...

● **Figure 5.4** An RSPB advertisement on behalf of bitterns.

The Woodland Trust own some 600 woods with a combined area of 8000 hectares. It has an annual income of £6 million and 150 000 active supporters. It has defined a set of woodland management principles 'in order to convey a clear understanding of the way in which we seek to manage our woods to all those who support our work'. These 11 woodland management principles are as follows.

1 The Woodland Trust invites its members and the general public into its woods for informal recreation and quiet enjoyment. Safety is paramount, and will be secured before any Trust woods are opened to visitors.

2 The Trust provides and maintains footpaths, gates, stiles and similar low-level facilities for public access to a level appropriate to the degree of use of each property.

3 The public benefit of the Trust's woods lies principally in their aesthetic qualities – beauty, tranquillity, timelessness – and in their value for wildlife.

4 *In caring for and conserving its woods, the primary aim of the Trust's silvicultural management is therefore to preserve these qualities by following and emulating natural processes as far as possible. This includes the retention, where appropriate, of old trees to full maturity and death.*

5 *Before taking any action the Trust considers carefully if it is necessary. The broadleaved timescale is measured in decades and there is very rarely any hurry to intervene.*

6 *If it is necessary to intervene the work will be as little and as unobtrusive as possible.*

7 *It is essential to understand clearly the long-term consequences of intervention and ensure that work is carried out in accordance with these principles.*

8 *Where we carry out any works in our woods we wish to achieve this in the most economical and effective manner possible but with full consideration of good woodland management practice.*

9 *The Trust does not make market-driven decisions but wherever possible costs of management operations will be minimised by imaginative and effective marketing.*

10 *We seek to explain our operations in advance and the support of the local community will be actively encouraged.*

11 *In assuming responsibility for the care of our woods in perpetuity, the Trust also recognises the obligations of ownership both as a landowner and as a neighbour.*

The Woodland Trust can be contacted at Autumn Park, Grantham, Lincolnshire NG31 6LL, UK (tel. 01476 74297).

The role of zoos in conservation

Zoos have three main aims: conservation, education and research. At the same time, zoos need to attract *people*. A zoo that fails to get enough people through its doors soon closes.

There was a time when zoos mainly bred animals because they knew the public would be attracted to the baby animals. Now almost every zoo, however small, has at least one **captive breeding programme** in which an endangered species is bred in captivity. Captive breeding programmes have the following benefits.

■ Fewer animals need to be caught in the wild and transported to zoos, thus reducing animal suffering.

■ Reduced pressure on the wild stock lessens the chances of extinction.

■ Successful captive breeding allows the possibility of the species being **reintroduced** into the wild.

A good example of captive breeding in action is the rescue of the Nene goose (*Branta sandvicensis*) (*figure 5.5*). This goose is the largest native bird of Hawaii. Here the birds clamber about on the sparsely vegetated, volcanic slopes. This hostile environment has resulted in the birds having larger toes and less webbing between the toes than other geese. It is less vocal than its mainland relatives, its call consisting of a low, mournful moan. In addition, uniquely among northern geese, the species is non-migratory.

During the nineteenth century there were probably over 20 000 Nene geese in the Hawaiian Archipelago. By the late 1940s there were only about 40. Their drastic decline was principally the result of the introduction of non-native terrestrial predators such as dogs, rats and mongooses. These animals found the Nene goose and its eggs easy prey. Ironically, the mongoose was only introduced in the hope that it would control the rats that had been introduced to the islands, but it became the biggest predator of the Nene goose.

In a desperate attempt to save the bird, two females and a male were sent, in 1951, to the **Wildfowl and Wetlands Trust** in England, founded

● *Figure 5.5* The Nene goose, rescued from extinction through captive breeding by the Wildfowl Trust.

by Sir Peter Scott in 1946. Initially breeding success was low, but with time better results were achieved and by the end of the 1970s there was a total of 1200 Nene geese in wildfowl sanctuaries around the world while some 1600 had been released back into Hawaii. Here they have successfully re-established themselves thanks to efforts to control the predators that attack them, such as putting wire netting around their nesting sites to stop the mongooses and rats getting to the eggs.

The Nene goose story is not unique. A number of other species have been rescued from extinction through captive breeding, including the golden lion tamarin (a small monkey found only in coastal forests of the state of Rio de Janeiro in Brazil) and the Arabian oryx (a large gazelle-like herbivore found in semi-desert scrub in the Middle East).

Despite these successes it must be realised that out of some 15 million different species of animal on Earth, a third are likely to be threatened with extinction by the year 2025. Captive breeding can only play a tiny part in helping to conserve all these animals.

Successful captive breeding is both an art and a science. For such programmes to work they need people with an excellent knowledge of the biology of the organism and people with perseverance and a love for the animal so that they keep going when little success seems to be forthcoming. Adequate funding is a necessity too.

Every captive breeding programme has to be aware of the problem of **inbreeding**. Inbreeding happens when closely related individuals, for example a brother and a sister, mate. Some species naturally inbreed in the wild. For these species, inbreeding in captivity poses few problems. However, most species only outbreed – so that parents are, at most, only distantly related. When these species inbreed, the offspring are much less likely to survive and reproduce successfully. The reason for this **inbreeding depression** is that inbreeding greatly increases the chances of an individual inheriting the same harmful recessive alleles from both parents. Offspring end up being homozygous for harmful recessive alleles at one or more of their genes. As a result, they may lack vital

gene products and be less likely to survive and reproduce successfully.

Because of the dangers of inbreeding, zoos nowadays keep careful records detailing the origin of all their animals. This allows them to ensure that individuals that mate are as distantly related as possible. Zoos often swap animals with other zoos to promote outbreeding. Encouraging outbreeding of individuals around the world also maintains the genetic diversity of the captive populations. Such diversity is important if groups of animals are eventually returned to the wild.

Captive breeding has a long-term value only if the habitats exist to re-introduce species. Is there a value in captive breeding if the populations remain in zoos for ever?

SAQ 5.1

Which sorts of species do members of the general public most want to see in zoos?

SAQ 5.2

Which sorts of species could zoos do most to help by captive breeding?

The role of botanic gardens in conservation

The earliest botanic gardens were created in China, in prehistoric Mexico and in the Arab world. The West followed much later, the first European botanic garden being founded in Pisa in 1543. In the sixteenth and seventeenth centuries the main function of European botanic gardens was to grow plants of medicinal value for the training of medical students. The focus of research then shifted to taxonomic studies in the eighteenth century. Today botanic gardens have many functions and conservation is an important one of them.

Botanic gardens can do a tremendous amount for conservation. While London Zoo houses only 900 species of animals, the Royal Botanic Gardens at Kew boast 50 000 of the world's 250 000 species of plants! It is easier and cheaper to keep a plant than an animal.

● *Figure 5.6* Part of the cold storage seed bank at Wellesbourne, Warwickshire.

One of the useful things about many plants is that their seeds can be kept alive for years *(figure 5.6)*. Careful reduction of the moisture content under conditions of low temperature, followed by freezing, preserves the seeds of most plants for many years, often for as long as two hundred years. Such **seed banks** play a vital role in conservation. Some seed banks specialise in preserving different varieties of crop plants. This maintains a gene reservoir for the breeding of future varieties.

The importance of seed banks in the conservation of crop varieties cannot be overestimated. The genetic uniformity of most of the world's food plants is very worrying. To date, disaster has largely been avoided through the application of huge quantities of pesticides. However, every few years much of the yield from one or other variety of wheat, potato, maize or other food crop is lost as a result of the evolution of a new strain of insect or fungus that can attack a particular crop variety. As many countries now rely on only a handful of crop varieties there is always the possibility that one year most of the harvest of an entire country might fail.

Some plants, including a number of important crops, produce seed only rarely or produce seed that can only be stored for a few weeks or months. For these species a seed bank is impractical. An alternative is to grow different varieties of the adult plants year after year, ensuring that pollination occurs only within the crop to keep it genetically pure. The problem with this approach is the space, time and effort involved. Crops kept in this way include cocoa, rubber, coconut, mango, cassava and yam.

Agriculture and conservation

In the UK, conservation and agriculture are often thought to be in perpetual conflict. In many ways this is unfair on farmers and country landowners, most of whom know vastly more about wildlife than the average town or city dweller, and many of whom care for and respect nature, having worked outdoors all their lives. At the same time, farming is a job and is subject to market forces, including economic ones. Indeed, one of the problems for farmers is the way in which their ground rules are changed every few years with the imposition of new UK legislation or the emergence of another set of EU directives. It should also be noted that, in real terms, farming incomes more than halved from the 1970s to the 1990s. Employment in agriculture continues to fall and suicide rates for farmers remain far above the national average.

Pesticides

Pesticides include **herbicides** (used against weeds), **insecticides** (used to kill insects) and **fungicides** (which kill fungi such as mildews and rusts). Pesticide application, the use of fertilisers and the introduction of new crop varieties, have been responsible for great increases in UK farm yields over the past fifty years. By their very nature pesticides are intended to kill organisms, so it is not surprising that their use can cause environmental and health problems.

Only occasionally does herbicide use cause problems. Most herbicides break down rapidly, being **biodegradable**, and are only poisonous to animals when absorbed or ingested at high concentrations. However, herbicide use has been responsible for a great reduction in the variety and number of wild plants seen on UK farmland. Even poppies are uncommon in many parts of the country, whilst a number of plants that were once serious agricultural weeds are now national rarities. These include such beautiful plants as corncockle (*Agrostemma githago*) with its large purple flowers and shepherd's-needle (*Scandix pecten-veneris*) with its delicate white petals and long, striking fruits.

Substances used as insecticides include **pyrethroids, organo-chlorines, organophosphates** and **carbamates**. More recently, **insect growth regulators** have been developed. These mimic the action of insect growth hormones and so disrupt the development of mature insects from larvae.

A common problem with many insecticides is that they do not kill only the intended insect, known as the **target species**. The insecticide often kills useful pollinating insects, or even predators and parasites of the target species. A farmer may become locked into an expensive cycle, being forced to spray more frequently and more extensively than was originally intended because the natural predators of the target species have been wiped out.

A second problem is that the target species may evolve *resistance* to the insecticide. Again, the farmer may respond by using ever-increasing dosages. A better strategy can be to switch to a different class of insecticide for a couple of years before switching back to the original one. This strategy allows the farmer to keep one step ahead of the insect.

A third problem with some insecticides is that they become concentrated in food chains. For example, **DDT** and other organochlorines are soluble in fat rather than in water. Because of this they tend to be stored in the fatty tissues of animals, rather than

excreted. As a result, the concentration of the insecticide within an animal builds up as the food chain is ascended *(figure 5.7)*.

The accumulation of DDT and other organochlorines can be dangerous. In the 1940s the number of peregrine falcons began to fall. Over the next twenty years their numbers halved. Careful research showed that the decline was due to the accumulation of organochlorine residues within the falcons. These caused the birds to lay eggs with thinner shells. As a result, the eggs were more likely to break before hatching. Eventually the British government introduced restrictions on the use of organochlorine insecticides. By the late 1980s peregrine falcon numbers were back to their former levels.

Certain inorganic chemicals have long been used as **fungicides**. Copper salts have been employed to protect grape vines against fungi for over a hundred years. More recently a number of organic fungicides, such as **zineb** and **benomyl**, have been developed. Fungicides are not known to cause many ecological problems.

Hedgerow removal

A **hedgerow** is a narrow belt of vegetation dominated by a variety of shrubs, sometimes with occasional trees. Hedgerows are the result of human activity. Their history is a fascinating and complex subject. Traditionally they served two functions: as a barrier to the movement of livestock, and as a means of marking out the boundaries of property.

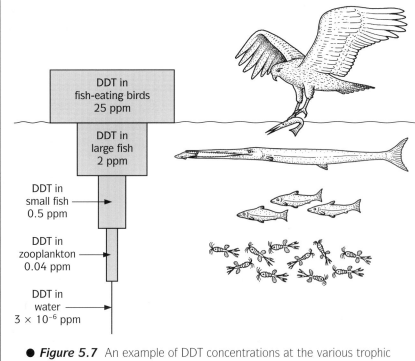

● *Figure 5.7* An example of DDT concentrations at the various trophic levels of an estuarine food chain.

Because so much of Britain lacks trees and is dominated by fields, hedgerows are of great ecological significance. They are a home for hundreds of animal and plant species and often act as essential wildlife corridors connecting scattered woods and copses. Amongst the best-known plants in British hedges are shrubs such as blackthorn, hawthorn and hazel, and smaller plants such as primrose, lords and ladies, hart's-tongue fern and garlic mustard. Vertebrates that live in hedges include the bank vole and birds such as the wren, hedge sparrow and yellowhammer. Invertebrates are numerous, including butterflies such as the brimstone, orange tip and hedge brown.

Unfortunately the large farm machinery in use today means that large fields are more profitable than small ones. Hedges are therefore seen to take up valuable space and are often removed. It is difficult to quantify the problem, but it is thought than from the end of the Second World War through to the 1980s approximately 8000 km of hedgerow were lost each year in the UK. More recently the loss has declined, though in 1993 the British conservation organisation Plantlife estimated that losses were still totalling 6000 km a year. Reasons for this slight decline in the rate of hedgerow removal include:

- the fact that many of the hedges that could be removed have already been;
- the fact that hedgerows have a beauty of their own is becoming more widely appreciated;
- the appreciation of research which has shown that hedgerows are habitats for pollinators of certain crops and for predators and parasites of many pests – removing hedgerows may therefore *reduce* crop yields;
- the realisation that hedgerow removal can increase soil erosion.

Drainage

Some land is naturally too wet to support crop plants and so is **drained**. Drainage has a number of benefits for the farmer. In particular, it prevents **waterlogging**. Waterlogging leads to anaerobic conditions which can kill many plants or, if less severe, slow down the plant's uptake of minerals by active transport. **Denitrification** is more common in waterlogged conditions, leading to the loss of nitrate from the soil. Waterlogged soils take longer to warm up in spring, so slowing the initial growth rate of certain crops, and can be difficult to manage with heavy farm machinery.

Although beneficial to the crop plants, drainage has greatly decreased the diversity of wildlife in Britain. Traditionally, meadows were cut only once a year – for hay – and so displayed a profusion of plant life which, in turn, supported many insects and other animals. Despite every effort by conservation organisations, these flower-rich meadows are still disappearing. Almost unbelievably, 98% of the area of wet meadows in existence at the end of the Second World War was destroyed over the next 50 years. Many were ploughed and drained. However, conversion to horse paddocks is now the fate of many small meadows in the English lowlands. Horse paddocks can be floristically diverse, but they support an entirely different community and, if overgrazed, very few species of flowering plants survive.

Soil erosion in the UK

In chapter 4 we saw how overgrazing can lead to desertification with consequent loss of soil (see page 43). Earlier in this chapter we mentioned that hedgerow removal could also lead to the loss of soil. Soil loss, known as **soil erosion**, is all too often a result of agricultural practices such as these.

Growing annual crops is especially likely to lead to soil erosion. This is because every year, harvesting leads to a time when the soil surface is bare and exposed to the elements. Ploughing may increase the potential for erosion by turning the soil over and making it less compact. When fields are sparsely vegetated, even modest amounts of rain or wind can lead to the loss of soil. Floods and storms can result in even greater losses (*figure 5.8*). Such soil loss is evident in the brown colour of almost any lowland UK river when it is particularly swollen with rainwater.

Loss of soil through wind is less of a problem in the UK, although in the fens of East Anglia many of the residents frequently recount tales about some neighbour's entire newly planted sugar beet crop

● *Figure 5.8* Flooding in Sussex in January 1994. At this time of year, when fields have little vegetation on them, flooding can lead to considerable volumes of agricultural soil being washed away.

being carried off in a dust storm. Records show that over the last century around two metres in depth of peat have been lost from most of East Anglian fenland in this way, and through oxidation.

There are causes of soil erosion other than agriculture. In many of the most scenic parts of Britain, the pressure of human feet has led to significant erosion. The natural vegetation disappears and unsightly, broad, muddy or stony paths appear. Anyone who has walked much in the countryside, whether on the flat or up mountains, will know this all too well. Blanket peat bogs in uplands such as the Pennines are particularly susceptible.

Natural soil formation is a very slow process which usually takes hundreds of years. It requires the accumulation of inorganic particles of clay, silt and sand which are blown or washed into the area and the addition of organic matter from the vegetation growing nearby. Reversing soil loss is very difficult in the short term and the only quick solution is to transport soil from another site to

the required area: a very large-scale and expensive process. The best solution is to prevent, or at least reduce, further erosion by improving agricultural practices and reducing trampling. The strength of winds, which carry dry soil particles away, can be lessened locally by the strategic planting of shelter-belt trees and hedges. Disturbed soil is particularly vulnerable, so it is best to plant crops with minimum soil disturbance (direct drilling) rather than widespread ploughing. A further problem with intensive agricultural practices is that many of the soil organisms which maintain soil structure, including arthropods and worms, are destroyed. This treatment damages the soil which often loses its drainage and water-holding properties, allowing erosion by surface water run-off in wet weather and dust blow in dry weather.

In natural vegetation the most obvious cause of erosion, from thousands of trampling boots, can be reduced by reinforcing pathways, ideally using natural materials. Paths in areas of high visitor pressure, such as the Lake District, Snowdonia and the Pennines, have been reinforced with stone. Peaty paths, which are usually widened by walkers trying to find dry footing, can be provided with wooden walkways across the wetter areas.

SUMMARY

In the UK, government protection for wildlife is mainly provided through the establishment of National Parks, National Nature Reserves and Sites of Special Scientific Interest.

Other UK government action to protect wildlife includes the designation of Environmentally Sensitive Areas, and the passing of the Wildlife and Countryside Act 1981 and other legislation.

Voluntary bodies, such as the Royal Society for the Protection of Birds and the Woodland Trust, play a vital role in conservation.

Zoos have three main aims: conservation, education and research. Nowadays most zoos have one or more captive breeding programmes as part of their conservation effort.

Among the animals saved by captive breeding and subsequent release are the Nene goose, golden lion tamarin and Arabian oryx. Captive breeding programmes usually have to be carefully planned to avoid inbreeding depression.

Botanic gardens can play a significant role in nature conservation, partly through the maintenance of seed banks. Seed banks can also be used to preserve the genetic diversity of crop varieties.

Agriculture and conservation need not be in opposition. Nevertheless, pesticide use, hedgerow removal, drainage and other agricultural practices can lead to a number of problems including soil erosion and loss of biodiversity.

Questions

1 Compare the aims, efforts and achievements of **government** and **voluntary** conservation organisations in the UK.

2 Argue the case **for** and **against** zoos.

3 Discuss the effects of agriculture on the UK countryside.

Chapter six

Local conservation

By the end of this chapter you should be able to:

1 discuss the issues involved in recycling;

2 list the ways in which an individual can influence conservation at local, national and international level;

3 compare the different ways we can affect our environment as consumers, preservers of existing habitats and creators of new habitats;

4 apply this knowledge to suggest how a local habitat could be maintained or improved for wildlife.

For your local area you need to do some research so that you:

5 know about the conservation measures of your local council;

6 are able to describe the work of your local wildlife trust.

In this chapter we shall investigate what are often called **green issues**. Usually people who apply the principle of conservation to their lives are described as being 'green'. Green issues make us aware of how we can each do something to improve our environment. Because local conservation issues vary depending on where you live in Britain, the self-assessment questions (SAQs) in this chapter have been replaced by Action Ideas for you to find out more about your local area and what can be done there for conservation.

Conservation begins at home

To someone living in Britain, conservation can be a rather depressing subject. Very little of our land is untouched by human influences: most is farmland; the woods have mostly been planted or managed for generations; and the upland moors are often burned to regenerate the heather for grouse to live in. Everywhere the rivers, rain and air are polluted and the effects of pesticides and fertilisers are widespread. The depression deepens if an international conservation magazine such as *Oryx* (the

publication of the Fauna and Flora Preservation Society) is read as it is often full of reports of failures – species under threat and habitat destruction – all over the world.

In fact *everyone* can make choices which affect the environment. We are part of a global community. Some decisions we take, such as those which may alter the CO_2 or ozone levels in the atmosphere, can affect the whole world. Other decisions may have a national effect, still others a more immediate impact on our local area. Even within our battered landscape there are many opportunities to help wildlife both by preserving or improving what remains and by constructing new areas where wildlife can thrive. Often it is only when enough people in society think something is valuable and do something about it that the authorities really take notice.

The ways in which an individual can influence conservation are by being a careful consumer, by helping to preserve habitats and by creating new areas for wildlife.

Consumers

We all **consume** a great deal in a year: food; water; washing materials; clothes; and energy in the form of heat, light and fuel. You can add to the list yourself. This gives each of us a huge amount of choice about what we buy and how we use it. We can ask many questions as we make these choices.

■ Is the packaging of this article wasteful – can I buy a refill pack?

■ Does this wood come from a renewable plantation or from a tropical forest?

■ Are these bulbs or orchids propagated from garden stock or dug up from the wild? (It was estimated that 100 000 000 bulbs and corms were dug up in Turkey for export in 1986!)

■ Does this aerosol emit CFCs?

■ Is there an alternative to slug pellets?

Should I keep tropical fish?

Is this petrol lead-free?

Can I find an alternative to bog peat for the garden? (Coconut fibre and cocoa seedcases are renewable resources.)

Is this cotton or paper unbleached?

Has this food been grown using a minimum of environment-damaging pesticides?

Is this paper recycled?

Which of these cans of tuna is dolphin friendly?

Have I left a light or radiator on needlessly?

Products which are designed to cause minimum damage to the environment during production or use are called **environmentally friendly**.

Recycling

Recycling is the reusing of products or materials which would otherwise be thrown away. It includes reusing items in their original form or sending them back (usually in large amounts) to a factory to be pulped or melted down and made into useful articles. Recycling takes a bit of effort but is something everyone can do. In 1989 the environmental organisation Friends of the Earth produced an **environmental charter** to guide local authorities on environmental issues. Part of the general aim was for an authority to 'seek to promote the conservation and sustainable use of natural resources and to minimise environmental pollution in all of its activities and through its influence over others'. Several councils signed the charter and many others adopted some of the more specific green aims in their own policies. Many city and county councils now produce leaflets stating their environmental policies for many issues such as pollution, water resources, transport and recycling.

A few councils provide door-to-door collection of recyclable material *(figure 6.1)*. Many more have collection points at convenient places (often car parks and supermarkets) where items such as bottles, paper, books, cans, some plastics, aluminium foil and textiles can be left by members of the public. They may also run extra services such as Christmas tree shredding and the collection of old refrigerators so that the ozone-damaging CFC coolants can be removed safely.

● *Figure 6.1* A collection lorry for the door-to-door blue box recycling scheme in Sheffield. Residents leave recyclable waste in large blue plastic boxes ready for collection and transportation to recycling units.

Recycling can save both the natural resources of the Earth and the energy used to manufacture new products. For example, 1 tonne of paper requires wood pulp from about 16 trees. Recycling paper therefore saves trees. Making an aluminium can from recycled material uses 20 times less energy than making a can from raw materials, as well as saving the natural environment in areas of the world where aluminium is mined.

Kitchen waste can be recycled by composting it and using it in the garden. Any material which is recycled or composted instead of thrown away decreases the volume of rubbish which goes into landfill sites where it is unsightly and produces methane (one of the greenhouse gases) during rotting. The UK government has set a target that, by the year 2000, 25% of all waste must be recycled.

ACTION IDEA 6.1

Find out what your local council's green policies are and what it is doing to promote recycling.

Reusing items in their original form is, in many ways, even better than remaking things because it saves the energy needed to reprocess the recycled materials. Often there are other benefits. Charities can raise money by selling donated clothing and other items, and unwanted clothing and blankets can benefit people in disaster areas.

Many things can be reused:

- returnable bottles (milk and some soft drinks);
- jars and bottles (which can be passed on to marmalade and wine makers);
- paper only used on one side, envelopes, cards and calendars (which can be used for gift tags or children's art classes);
- clothes in good condition (which can be used by charities);
- plastic carrier bags.

Saving energy

Energy consumption in the UK is high. Unfortunately most of our energy comes from the burning of fossil fuels – coal, oil and gas. Electricity generation is particularly wasteful as electricity is usually produced from fossil fuels and then turned back into heat and light in the home. (Every time energy is transformed from one form to another some energy is lost, so the more conversion processes there are the more energy is wasted.) As all these fuels produce CO_2 and other harmful gases (e.g. sulphur dioxide), they are not 'green'. But is there an environmentally friendly fuel?

Nuclear power is clean and does not release CO_2, but it can hardly be considered friendly if there is a radiation leak. Sheep in some parts of Britain were still eating radioactive grass years after the large radiation leak from Chernobyl in the Ukraine in 1986.

Wave power is also clean, but the construction of large devices to catch the waves' energy can damage coastal habitats if not sensitively placed. Wind power is effective, but some people think that huge modern windmill farms are unsightly in the countryside. Solar panels seem a good idea, but the amount of heat they can generate is rather unpredictable in the UK because of the cloudy weather we so often have.

Wood-burning stoves are also ecologically sound. Although burning releases CO_2 the wood is a **renewable resource** not a fossil fuel. Medieval woods (like the one in *figure 6.2*) were managed for many products. Straight oak trees were allowed to grow tall so that their wood could be used as structural timber for houses and ships. The smaller trees of the undergrowth such as hazel and ash were **coppiced**, that is cut down to ground level, and allowed to regrow for several years before harvesting. The resulting tall straight poles were used for fencing, house walls ('wattle and daub'), kindling and firewood. Many of these remaining old woods have fallen into disuse, but conservationists are now coppicing them again. Unfortunately we do not have enough woodland to supply everyone in the UK with wood to burn, but there are now some wood-burning power stations which are generating electricity for the National Grid.

Using rubbish as a fuel, by burning it in an incinerator and then supplying houses in the area with heat, reduces fossil fuel consumption *and* solves the problem of rubbish disposal in landfill sites. In Sheffield, for example, 3500 homes are heated by the council incinerator. This has saved the release of over 40 000 tonnes of CO_2 from fossil fuel since it was set up.

Although most of us can do little to change the type of energy we use, we *can* change how much we use. Saving energy also makes our fuel bills smaller. There are many energy-saving devices

● **Figure 6.2** This ancient wood, Hayley Wood in Cambridgeshire, was being coppiced for poles and firewood 750 years ago. The tall trees are oak and ash while the coppiced stools, which have just been cut close to the ground, are hazel and ash.

from the expensive, such as double glazing, to the relatively cheap, such as energy efficient long-lasting light bulbs. It is quite surprising how changes which seem trivial can make a large difference when added up all over the country. For example, many people only switch off their TVs at night by remote control, which does not completely turn the TV off. To make this extra electricity, extra fossil fuel has to be burned at the power stations. It is estimated that 200 000 tonnes of CO_2 a year are released into the atmosphere because of this practice! A 1 °C reduction in the temperature of a house can save fuel (and therefore reduce fuel bills) by up to 8 %; an empty roof rack on a car increases petrol consumption by about 8 % too.

Preserving what is there

It is true that, compared to many countries, the UK is poor in natural, unspoiled habitats, but we do still have much diversity – woodlands, blanket and raised peat bogs, lowland heaths, salt marshes and chalk grassland. Good-quality habitats, especially ancient ones with a long history, are extremely valuable yet declining in number. Habitats such as ancient coppiced woodland and water meadows have taken thousands of years to develop rich floras and faunas. If they are destroyed they can never be recreated. Like smashing a favourite vase, even if it is glued together again the cracks will still be there. Our ancient woodland (*figure 6.2*) has shrunk from 1650 kha in 1086 (when it was recorded for the Domesday book) to 600 kha in 1890 and just 300 kha in 1980.

As was mentioned in chapter 5 (page 53) voluntary bodies play an important role in conservation in the UK. Often they can only ensure the preservation of a habitat by buying it to manage as a reserve: the government legislation is not strong enough to trust. Too many development schemes for roads, houses and so on are allowed to damage the valuable remaining sites. At least 5 % of SSSIs are damaged every year. The aims and work of two voluntary societies, the RSPB and the Woodland Trust, were described in detail in chapter 5.

Another nationwide conservation body is the Wildlife Trusts Partnership, collectively known as the **Royal Society for Nature Conservation** (RSNC). This is one of the major voluntary organisations and is made up of 47 local Wildlife Trusts and 50 Urban Wildlife Groups. Total membership exceeds 250 000 people. The RSNC runs major projects such as the Environment City Project on **sustainability**. This has been investigating ways in which human communities can take action to recycle and live in a way which does not deplete the world's resources. Using wood or rubbish or solar power to heat homes is an example of sustainability.

The address of the central office of the RSNC is The Green, Witham Park, Waterside South, Lincoln, LN5 7JR, UK (tel: 01522 544400).

Because these naturalist societies are voluntary they rely on funding from the general public to be able to carry out their programmes of conservation. There are many ways you can help such societies. You can become a member, visit the local reserves, take part in fundraising, do surveys of plants and animals and even, if the opportunity arises, help to manage a reserve.

The **British Trust for Conservation Volunteers** (BTCV) is a useful group to contact if you are interested in getting actively involved in conservation. They run hundreds of practical courses each year on topics such as dry-stone walling, hedge laying and pond cleaning, as well as providing working holidays for over 16s. They also run a school membership scheme giving advice about conservation in school grounds. The BTCV has contacts and local offices in almost every county, but their main office is The British Trust for Conservation Volunteers, 36 St Mary's Street, Wallingford, Oxfordshire, OX10 0EU, UK (tel: 01491 839766).

The **RSPB** organises annual bird surveys such as the Big Garden Birdwatch: individuals can take part by watching their garden or a nearby area on the appointed day to see which bird species visit. The changes in abundance of different bird species from year to year can give vital information about which birds are thriving and which might be in danger of decline. Some birds, such as starlings, seem to thrive in the urban environment while others, like thrushes, are doing less well.

Other surveys enlisting the help of individuals all over Britain have included rook watches, National Dormouse Week (hunts for nuts opened by dormice), otter surveys and a survey of what cats catch. (The threat to wildlife from some domestic cats is considerable.)

ACTION IDEA 6.2

Find out what your local Wildlife Trust is called and where its reserves are in your area. Visit one to see how it is managed.

Improving our environment

Much of our land could support abundant wildlife, but it has been spoiled by the use of fertilisers, insecticides, fungicides and herbicides. The picture that may spring to mind when all these are mentioned is of large agricultural fields, but many streams and rivers, glasshouses, orchards, recreation areas and gardens have the same problems caused by chemical overuse.

Unfortunately all these chemical applications not only help the crops to grow by killing pests, they also kill harmless organisms and even beneficial predators. Such predators would keep down the numbers of pests naturally by **biological control**, reducing the need for so many pesticides. In fact pesticides are sometimes so damaging to predators that they may even allow the pest to increase! If you look at *figure 6.3* you can see the effect of spraying DDT on a crop of brassicas (e.g. cabbages and Brussels sprouts) in an attempt to control the cabbage white butterfly. After three lots of spraying, more butterfly eggs were found on the crops than in an unsprayed control area. The soil-dwelling predators of the cabbage white butterfly had been killed by long-lasting poisonous DDT residues in the soil. On the sprayed crop, 70% of the eggs laid by cabbage white butterflies survived, while only 40% survived on the unsprayed crop because the predators were still there to eat the eggs. DDT use is now restricted because of its harmful effects on wildlife (see page 58), but even replacement insecticides may have a similar effect. In

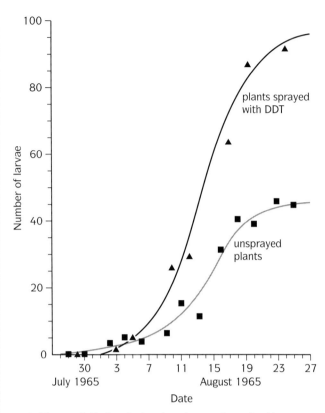

● *Figure 6.3* Graph showing the number of cabbage white butterfly larvae on 64 brassica plants during summer 1965. The 32 sprayed plants had DDT applications on 6 July and 20 August 1964, then again on 28 July 1965.

other words, sometimes it is not only better for the environment, but also better and cheaper for the farmer, not to resort to pesticides.

The urban environment

About 80% of people in the UK live in **urban areas**. Urban areas contain a number of habitats which are suitable for wildlife: gardens, verges, railway embankments, canals, sewage treatment plants, parks, golf courses, football pitches, churchyards and cemeteries, vacant and derelict land. Even derelict areas can be upgraded to form wildlife havens (*figure 6.4*) and these places make excellent havens for humans too.

There are 26 SSSIs in London. The parks of London are also famous for their wildlife – for example Regents Park has a colony of herons and 100 native species of butterflies and moths. Similarly, Sutton Park in Birmingham has 400 species of flowering plant, 27 of which are found nowhere else in Warwickshire. Even a truly urban microhabitat – the wall – can be a rich place for wildlife. In a survey of Cambridge city (which, it must be admitted, has an unusually abundant supply of old, mellow brick and stone walls) 178 flowering plant species and 7 fern species, as well as many mosses and algae, were found growing on walls.

With sensitivity from local councils, great improvements can be made to wildlife habitats in and around urban areas. Urban nature sites are especially important because of their value as recreation areas. Most people feel fulfilled by contact with nature – they enjoy feeding birds or sitting under a tree. Areas valuable both for humans and wildlife can be created, with a bit of effort, even in the largest urban sprawls. *Figure 6.5* shows the plan of an urban park in Stoke-on-Trent. This land was once derelict tips of colliery spoil, but has been made into a park with areas for games and sport as well as a lake, meadows and woods.

● *Figure 6.4* The Jupiter Urban Wildlife Project started in 1990 to transform an area of disused railway sidings in industrial Grangemouth, Scotland into a wildlife garden with ponds, woods and flowerbeds.
  a Landscaping on the site early in 1992.
  b A profusion of wildflowers in summer 1993.

In the garden

Gardens can be a haven for wildlife if they are not too heavily tainted with pesticides and pollutants and are not too tidy! A garden can easily be upgraded for wildlife by going organic. That includes relying on biological controls to keep the pests down. Hedgehogs, toads and thrushes can kill slugs and snails as efficiently as slug pellets. Some slug pellets harm wildlife and domestic pets which eat them. As mentioned earlier, the RSPB surveys of garden birds show that thrushes have declined in number. There were only about half the number of song thrushes seen in the 1994 survey compared with 1979! This is probably mainly due to a lack of food (slugs and snails) in over-controlled gardens and farmland.

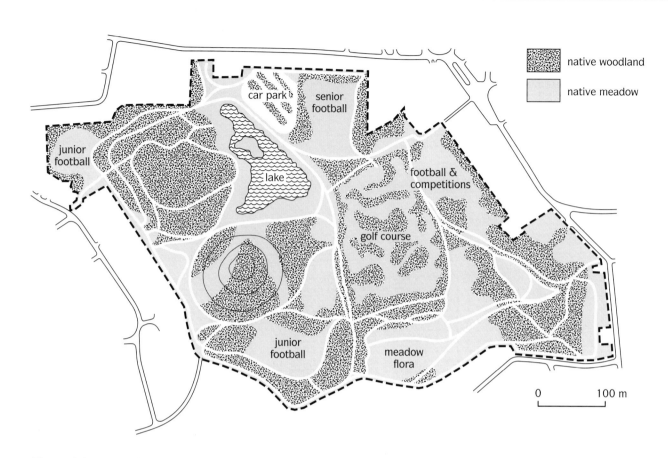

● **Figure 6.5** Plan of Central Forest Park in Stoke-on-Trent, UK which was constructed on derelict colliery spoil tips between 1969 and 1974.

Ladybirds and hoverfly larvae are great eaters of aphids (known to gardeners as greenfly and blackfly) and this natural system of control improves the longer the garden is unsprayed. Only a few garden plants (but especially roses) ever get bad attacks of aphids and the main cause is ants. Ants 'farm' aphids and collect the nutritious sticky fluids they excrete. Because they are valuable to the ants, the aphids are protected from attack by ant 'guards' so that predators are unable to eat many. Ants are not so easy to get rid of organically, but they are fascinating creatures to have around!

Composted kitchen waste can be used instead of manufactured fertilisers, or, for those very greedy vegetables, an organic fertiliser made from chicken manure or cow dung can be bought in.

Increasing the variety of habitats in a garden is also important. Compost heaps or piles of leaves may be used by hibernating hedgehogs (check your bonfire in autumn before lighting it in case you have

a visitor) and may even be used by grass snakes to lay their eggs in if you are lucky. Leave some old wood in a sheltered corner for insects, woodlice and millipedes to live in or under. Other possible improvements include adding features like those suggested under the heading 'Creating new habitats' (page 69).

Providing nestboxes for roosting or breeding animals to use can be very rewarding. Even a small garden can hold a bird box for small breeding birds such as wrens, blue tits or great tits. Bat boxes can be put up for bats to **roost** (sleep) in during the day. Some quite rare species have been encouraged to use nesting boxes, including barn owls and dormice. Some nests which are put up can be quite bizarre: long-eared owls will nest in open wicker baskets nailed high in trees, while harvest mice can be encouraged to visit and nest in old, specially waterproofed tennis balls, with a small hole in the front, on 40 cm-high sticks baited with budgie or finch seed! *Figure 6.6* illustrates the

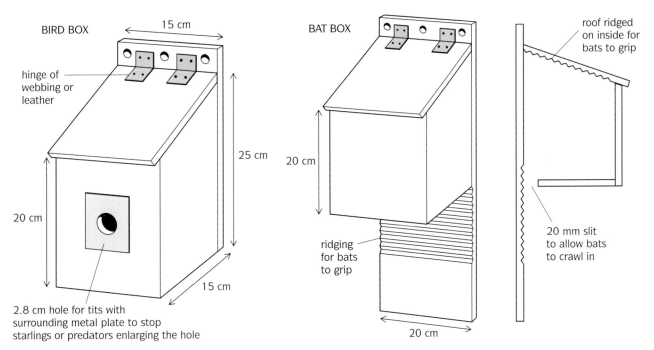

● *Figure 6.6* Diagrams of nesting and roosting boxes for birds and bats, showing the dimensions needed for construction. Remember not to use timber treated with preservative containing fungicides as these can harm the animals.

dimensions of a small bird nesting box and a bat roosting box.

Many animals can be encouraged into the garden by providing food. Some food sources are natural, such as plant species which butterflies visit for nectar or on which they lay their eggs. Other foodstuffs can be provided from the kitchen. Hedgehogs love cat food (bread and milk are not really good for them) and there are even some hedgehog foods for sale from wildlife food suppliers. A variety of birds can also be supported during the winter and early spring on peanuts and sunflower seeds (tits especially), old crunched-up biscuits and seeds mixed in fat (try to keep the starlings away) and special softbill food (for robins and blackbirds).

Churchyards

Churchyards may be either urban or rural. They are often very rich places for wildlife because they are relatively quiet and undisturbed, they often have mature trees in them and they possess a variety of stone substrates (some very interesting lichens can be found on gravestones).

Many churchyards are, however, kept extremely neat and tidy, with very short-mown grass and no weeds. Most churchyards could probably benefit (for wildlife's sake) from a **management plan**. It is always important to remember that people visiting graves can be very distressed by an unkept appearance to the grounds so usually it is best to keep the grass short round recent graves and restrict longer grass (mown only in very early spring and late summer) to more secluded areas. In one rural churchyard evidence of nesting harvest mice was found only two years after the introduction of a management plan which provided long summer grass in some quiet areas of the church grounds. Moles, too, can thrive in church grounds. Tree planting in churchyards can also increase the attraction for wildlife and will enhance the place for visitors too, especially if attractive native species such as wild cherry, silver birch, yew and spindle tree are planted.

Creating new habitats

Although it was mentioned earlier that some habitats, such as ancient woodland and water meadows, cannot really be replaced once destroyed, it is still possible to do a lot of good for the local flora and fauna by **creating new habitats** in impoverished areas. Suitable places for adding new, quality environments for wildlife include farmland that has been set aside (see page 53), school grounds, private gardens and derelict land.

Plant a tree

One tree can provide micro-habitats for a large number of small animals and even the most impoverished of school grounds probably has room for one. Of course a whole wood would be even better, but few of us have the opportunity to plant a wood.

Tree species	Number of insect species
Native trees	
oaks	284
willow	266
birch	229
hawthorn	149
sloe (blackthorn)	109
poplar	97
apple	93
Scots pine	91
alder	90
ash	41
hornbeam	28
rowan	28
yew	1
Introduced trees	
spruce	37
fir	16
sycamore	15
horse chestnut	4
walnut	3
acacia	1
plane	0

● **Table 6.1** The number of insect species found on trees growing in Britain

The choice of tree, especially if only one or two can be planted, is actually quite important. Certain trees are **native** to this country, that is they invaded the British Isles naturally, after the last Ice Age. Some (like pine and birch) invaded very soon after the ice melted, while others (like lime and hornbeam) came later. Some trees have been **introduced** into Britain, that is they are not native trees but normally live in other parts of the world. A number of the trees with which we are most familiar, including sycamore and horse chestnut, have actually been introduced. Introduced trees have fewer animal species living on them, possibly because their native fauna was left behind or does not thrive in Britain and the British animals have not evolved to use them.

Table 6.1 gives the number of insect species that live on some of our native trees and some of our introduced ones. As you can see, the native trees usually have many more insect species on them. It is always more ecologically sound to plant a native species. You could choose a tree which can support a large number of insects, or one which provides seeds and fruit for other wildlife. Jays and squirrels collect acorns from oaks for their winter stores, and birds such as the blackbird enjoy eating rowan berries in autumn.

Dig a pond

Water is very important for wildlife. Not so long ago many farms had more wetland areas, water meadows and temporary or perma-nent ponds. Artificial drainage coupled with severe droughts in many years (1990, 1991 and 1992 for example) in some parts of Britain have had disastrous effects on populations of aquatic and semi-aquatic animals. Frogs, newts and toads have declined in numbers in many places. A pond can be surprisingly rich in wildlife and a very rewarding habitat to add to a garden or open area. Even a very small pond has a wildlife value.

Small ponds can be lined with a flexible butyl lining laid on a layer of sand or newspapers (so that sharp stones do not pierce the lining when the weight of water is added). Very large ponds may need professional help as they often require a layer of concrete or a thick clay lining (puddled clay) to hold the water. *Figure 6.7* shows a section through a small pond with some suggested plants. It is always best to try to obtain native species for wildlife habitats. However, a garden pond can still be a valuable place for wildlife even with nursery-cultivated plants. For a very small pond, for example, the native water-lilies and rushes are often too large and vigorous, so smaller cultivated varieties may be more suitable. As long as these species aerate the pond and provide food for the animals it is not so important that they are native species. If the project was to put a large pond in a reclaimed land area or reserve then native species would, of course, be much better than garden varieties.

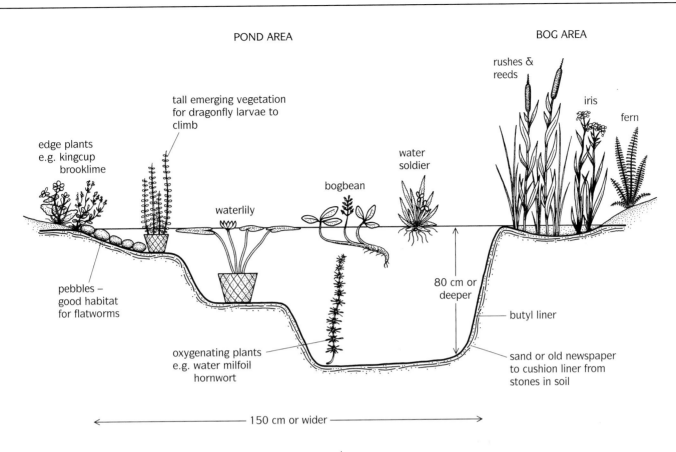

POND AREA   BOG AREA

rushes &
reeds

iris

fern

tall emerging vegetation
for dragonfly larvae to
climb

edge plants
e.g. kingcup
brooklime

water
soldier

bogbean

waterlily

pebbles –
good habitat
for flatworms

80 cm or
deeper

butyl liner

oxygenating plants
e.g. water milfoil
hornwort

sand or old newspaper
to cushion liner from
stones in soil

150 cm or wider

● **Figure 6.7** Section through a pond showing the
general layout and suitable plants.

One of the exciting aspects of a pond is that it
can be planted with vegetation and then left for
animals to invade on their own. It is not unknown
for a diving water-beetle to arrive at a pond as it is
being filled with water (although such an early
arrival is unlikely to stay as there is nothing as yet
for it to eat!). Even modest ponds can have
resident frogs or newts and breeding dragonflies
within one or two years. Dragonfly larvae live
underwater and are voracious predators; they are
fascinating to watch as they finally climb out onto
nearby tall vegetation to turn into large, winged
adult dragonflies.

Perhaps one of the major 'don'ts' for a pond is
do not have goldfish or any other exotic fish
species. They will eat many of the wild invertebrate species you are hoping to attract. Do dig the
pond as deep as you can so that some water is safe
from freezing in winter and drying up in hot
summers. Always put in as large a pond as you can.

Add a hedgerow

Hedges do not have to be restricted to farmland.
The Bass West Midlands Hedgerows Campaign
was launched by the Urban Wildlife Trust and the
local wildlife trust for Birmingham and the Black
Country in 1992. Since then, thousands of metres
of new hedge have been planted and several metro-
politan authorities in the area have signed a Hedge
Pledge to support hedgerows. Hedgerows in built-
up areas can be very important links, called
wildlife corridors, along which wildlife can travel
safely between larger green areas such as woods.

Hedgerows can, of course, be all shapes, sizes
and lengths: there is a hedgerow to suit all situa-
tions. The simplest is a single row of bushes. Then
there can be a double row up to a metre apart
(many nineteenth-century hedges were double
rows). The most complex includes a parallel ditch
and bank (made from the soil from the ditch) as
illustrated in *figure 6.8*. Such complex hedge and
ditch constructions provide a wide range of
habitats, including moist shade in the ditch, the

hedge itself and the extra area of sloping bank below the hedge.

Hedges are usually made of hawthorn with a number of additional tree, bush and climber species such as hazel, holly, ash, dog rose, honeysuckle and bramble. In Britain, some 16 species of bird and 14 species of mammal are known to breed in hedgerows (see *table 6.2*). Hedges are also

home to many molluscs (slugs and snails), beetles, gall wasps and spiders. Some of the plant species they naturally contain are listed in *figure 6.8*.

This brings us to a problem which was discussed earlier with respect to small garden ponds – that is, which species to plant and how much to plant or leave for natural invasion. Any nature reserve manager, even in the largest and most important reserves, faces this sort of problem, especially if a new feature is added. However, a hedgerow is a constructed, not a natural, habitat, so the basic structure of the hedge (the hawthorns) must be planted. Even then a new hedgerow will take time – about 20 years – to reach an adequate size and shape. The question is, should more species be added or should the plants be left to invade by natural succession?

Studies of old hedges show that on average, one new woody species invades a 30 m length of hedge every 100 years. Many species in the banks of

Bird species	Mammal species
hedge sparrow	wood mouse
house sparrow	field vole
wren	common vole
robin	bank vole
blackbird	common shrew
song thrush	pygmy shrew
blue tit	brown rat
great tit	hedgehog
long-tailed tit	mole
chaffinch	rabbit
bullfinch	stoat
greenfinch	weasel
goldfinch	fox
linnet	badger
yellowhammer	
wood pigeon	

● **Table 6.2** Animals which breed in hedgerows in Britain

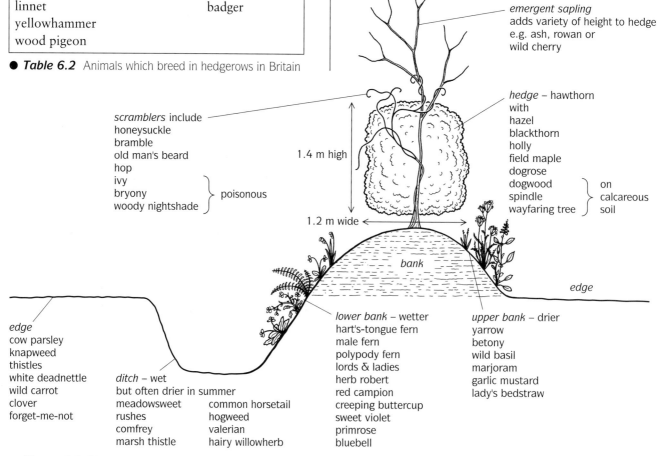

scramblers include
honeysuckle
bramble
old man's beard
hop
ivy
bryony ⎫
woody nightshade ⎭ poisonous

1.4 m high

1.2 m wide

emergent sapling
adds variety of height to hedge
e.g. ash, rowan or
wild cherry

hedge – hawthorn
with
hazel
blackthorn
holly
field maple
dogrose
dogwood ⎫
spindle ⎬ on calcareous soil
wayfaring tree ⎭

bank

edge

edge
cow parsley
knapweed
thistles
white deadnettle
wild carrot
clover
forget-me-not

ditch – wet
but often drier in summer
meadowsweet   common horsetail
rushes   hogweed
comfrey   valerian
marsh thistle   hairy willowherb

lower bank – wetter
hart's-tongue fern
male fern
polypody fern
lords & ladies
herb robert
red campion
creeping buttercup
sweet violet
primrose
bluebell

upper bank – drier
yarrow
betony
wild basil
marjoram
garlic mustard
lady's bedstraw

● **Figure 6.8** Diagram of a hedge and ditch showing what might be planted to create a new habitat.

ancient hedgerows such as bluebell, primrose and dog's mercury are remnants of woodland that was once there and will hardly ever colonise a new hedge. Waiting for succession would be a long job, and for the sake of the more mobile wildlife such as bees, mice and birds, it is probably best to plant up the banks and the hedge itself with a variety of species.

So where should the plants come from? Wild stock, that is plants similar to those in the area where the hedge is to grow, will be better than plants from a garden centre. Populations of plants growing in different areas of Britain have slight variations in appearance and character (such as flowering time). But it is illegal to dig up any native plant without the permission of the landowner where it grows. Even if such permission is granted it is better to leave such plants where they are growing rather than uproot them for a new site. However, digging up plants (with permission) would be justified if they are being rescued from a hedgerow that is about to be destroyed. Wild species could be bought from specialist plant nurseries, but an alternative, which takes a little longer but is far more satisfying in the end, is to grow the herbaceous plants yourself from local seed.

Seed can be gathered from nearby hedgerows in autumn. This way you not only get to know your local hedge flora, but you also get plants with a genetic range suitable to your area. It is a good idea to always leave some seed behind on each plant you gather from so that every plant has at least some seed to shed into the environment.

SUMMARY

- Individuals can contribute to international, national and local conservation.

- As consumers we can all choose whether or not to buy environmentally friendly products and save energy.

- Many items such as glass, cans, paper, clothes and some plastics can be recycled or reused.

- Some energy sources – solar power (captured by solar panels), wind power, wave power and nuclear power – do not release CO_2 into the atmosphere. Wood does but, because harvested woodland regrows and takes in CO_2, wood is a renewable resource.

- The Wildlife Trusts Partnership (RSNC) manages a large number of reserves to conserve habitats and wildlife.

- Some crop pests can be controlled by biological control rather than by the use of pesticides.

- There are many places where wildlife can survive in urban areas. Gardens can be particularly valuable if wildlife is encouraged by the provision of food, nestboxes and suitable habitats, and by avoiding pesticides.

- Creating new habitats such as woods, ponds and hedgerows is particularly important in order to increase the abundance and range of many species.

Questions

1 Describe how recycling can save the Earth's resources. With reference to your own local authority, discuss the difficulties of setting up a recycling scheme in your area.

2 What are the problems of managing small nature reserves in the UK? Discuss the importance of **a named reserve** near your home.

Answers to self-assessment questions

Chapter 1

1.1 Biome, ecosystem, community, habitat, microhabitat.

1.2 Nutrient status (especially nitrate and phosphate levels), pH, oxygen content and changes in oxygen during the year, light penetration, depth, size, temperature, temperature range (daily and annual), muddiness of water, physical characteristics of the bottom and sides (e.g. whether mud, sand or rock), whether freshwater or salty, whether closed (no streams/rivers entering/leaving) or open, whether sides are steep or gradually sloped.

1.3 *Either* find cowpats of different ages *or* watch a number of cowpats from soon (hours) after being deposited by cows. Make measurements of physical environment and how this changes during the succession (e.g. moisture levels, amount of organic matter). Catalogue succession of colonising species (e.g. different fungi, dung flies and other invertebrates). Work out how long it takes for the cowpat to 'disappear' and for the underlying habitat (grassland) to return to its previous state. Consider how different weather (rain, drought, frost) might alter results.

Chapter 2

2.1 Doubling time during exponential growth is between 4 and 6 months. Carrying capacity is between 8000 and 10 000 individuals.

2.2 The average number of eggs laid by each of the remaining females should increase, possibly by a factor of two (i.e. twice as many eggs laid by each remaining female).

2.3 The total number of eggs laid by the females should remain approximately the same (i.e. as many eggs laid in total by the females left as by all the females had none been removed).

Chapter 3

3.1 Increasing the size of the quadrat used would increase the species frequency.

3.2 a The population size will be underestimated.
b The population size will be overestimated.
c The population size will be overestimated.
d The population size will be overestimated.
e The population size will be underestimated.
f The population size will be overestimated.

Chapter 4

4.1 Ethical (elephants have a right to live). Valuable products from elephants (ivory, meat, elephant hide). Aesthetic (elephants beautiful, give pleasure to people). Tourist income. Role played by elephants in ecosystem.

4.2 Annual increase in the amount of carbon in the atmosphere is 3×10^{15} g. There are approximately 6 billion people (but you could also use 5.5 billion). So annual increase per person is equal to 3×10^{15} g divided by $6 \times 10^9 = 5 \times 10^5$ g, or approximately half a tonne.

4.3 Tax petrol/cars, encourage car sharing, provide good public transport, allow wood-burning stoves in smokeless zones, give grants for double glazing and roof insulation, encourage industries to use wind or water power, fund research on alternative energy sources, support a 'work at home' culture, give out free brochures on energy saving in the home, legislate so all new houses are designed to save energy.

Chapter 5

5.1 Mammals, especially large ones, rare ones or cute ones.

5.2 Small animals, inbred animals and endangered species whose habitats are under pressure.

Index (Numbers in italics refer to figures.)